T0282829

Endangered Virtues
and the Coming
Ideological War

A CHALLENGE FOR AMERICANS TO RECLAIM THE
HISTORIC VIRTUES OF THE NATION'S CHRISTIAN ROOTS

Michael Phillips

FIDELIS
PUBLISHING

FIDELIS PUBLISHING ®
ISBN: 9781956454444
ISBN (eBook): 9781956454451

Endangered Virtues and the Coming Ideological War:
A Challenge for Americans to Reclaim the Historic Virtues of the Nation's Christian Roots

Cover Design by Diana Lawrence
Interior Layout Design/Typesetting by Lisa Parnell
Edited by Lisa Parnell

Order at www.faithfultext.com for a significant discount. Email info@fidelispublishing.com to inquire about bulk purchase discounts.

Fidelis Publishing, LLC Sterling, VA • Nashville, TN fidelispublishing.com

Manufactured in the United States of America

10 9 8 7 6 5 4 3 2 1

TO:

My friend of many years
who suggested a nonfiction book to accompany
my fiction series, *Tribulation Cult*,
which was then in process.
Without his encouragement and gentle goading,
this book would never have been written.
I thank you, my friend!

A man of truth and virtue,
Nick Harrison

CONTENTS

Part 2 — Disengaged Engagement Strategies

ACKNOWLEDGMENTS

I am greatly appreciative to my "committee of advisors," more appropriately and truly *friends,* who read, added, suggested, edited, questioned, critiqued, and in myriad ways helped hone this book and its ideas into its final form. My multitude of counselors always adds wisdom to my life and efforts, exactly as Solomon said. I am grateful beyond measure to those who read the manuscript and offered comments, mentioning them in no particular order: George Yacoubian, Clarence Nason, Lora Hattendorf, Aaress Lawless, Michael Kimball, Joseph Dindinger, again Nick Harrison and his wife Beverly, of course my own wife Judy Phillips, along with one who requested to remain anonymous because of his daily professional involvement in the ideological wars. Preeminent among the rest is also publisher Gary Terashita, who believed in this book and who, with Nick, helped guide it from vision to reality.

The principles of this book explain why:

» words that have had clear meanings for thousands of years are suddenly being redefined in the most bizarre and illogical ways—and no one objects.

» it is now considered principled, even virtuous, for certain groups in our society to break laws, while others are ostracized, sued, even arrested for breaking no law except political correctness—and the media does not object.

» those with different cultural viewpoints are held to different legal standards depending on whether those viewpoints come from the Right or the Left—and few in the legal profession object.

» new forms of intolerance, fanaticism, cruelty, illegality, and discrimination are becoming widespread against those of a conservative worldview and why such practices are protected and praised—and secularists do not object.

» reverse-racism is not condemned but is encouraged as beneficial for society—and no one objects.

» the slaughter of unborns is permissible—and legions of progressives cheer.

» traditional Christian standards of right and wrong are excoriated as bigoted and hateful, while woke standards of hatefulness, injustice, prejudice, and favoritism are acclaimed as enlightened—and the champions of justice do not object.

» judgmentalism, narrow-mindedness, hate speech, bias, and religiophobia are considered virtuous as long as they are directed against conservatives—and liberals do not object.

» history may judge this generation of Americans to have been a population of lemmings that lost the capacity to think judiciously, logically, and implicationally.

» this nation is at a cultural and moral crossroads and is rapidly approaching a point of no return.

Introduction

A CROSSROADS OF VIRTUE

In recent years it is with grave concern that I have watched the rapid changes taking place in America and throughout the world. I believe, as do many, that as a people we are increasingly engaged in an ideological tug of war that will determine our future and that of generations to come.

Battle lines are being drawn. On one side are those pushing for changes that conflict with and often repudiate traditional American values. On the other side are those who cherish those same values even as they see them slipping away. They are convinced that essential to our continued national strength and identity is the reaffirmation, not the discarding, of values that have made America the exceptional nation it is.

Everyone realizes that change occurs as the future unfolds. Change *itself* is not intrinsically a bad thing. But which changes are beneficial and which are destructive? Which should we accept and which should we reject? What are the undergirding principles that give substance to the freedoms, and the democratic and spiritual ideals, upon which the United States was founded?

The battle over such questions is ideological. It is a conflict over the direction of a future in which truth and virtue are at stake. A time is coming when each of us will have to ask which side of the battle line we are on. Where will we stand as absolute truth and virtue become increasingly endangered commodities within the American landscape?

Discourse about cultural topics is inevitably divisive. As one who values unity as what ought to be among mankind's paramount priorities, I have tried to avoid controversy in my writing. Even in the rare instances when bold thinking has required wading gently into areas that might stir up debate, I have tried to approach the subjects cautiously and as objectively as possible. Controversy here will be inevitable. Yet the crumbling of our values is too important not to address.

When it comes to the cultural issues dividing us, large, sweeping, group virtues are at stake as well as those of a more personal nature. Even national virtue, of course, must be lived by individuals. All virtue is personal. But some virtues, taken collectively, determine the course of a nation's future.

We have to be wise thinkers to properly absorb and respond intelligently to the important idea-crisis that is overtaking us. We cannot take ideas haphazardly as they come, catching them, as the late Christian author and philosopher Francis Schaeffer once said, like measles. We have to be aware of how we think, aware of our presuppositions and worldviews, and the implications of both. Too much is at stake to be sloppy thinkers.

The changes inundating Americans are far more than political. There will always be opinionated debate (whom one should vote for, how much should we be taxed). Christians are Democrats and Republicans and everything else. Americans have been debating politics since John Adams and Thomas Jefferson squared off.

But something different is going on in the third millennium. The changes we are now witnessing in the public discourse contain a significant *spiritual* component in an increasingly hostile world. During the first two decades of the 2000s, the general culture in America grew decidedly less religious. More specifically, it became anti-*Christian*. In certain spheres (academia, high-tech, and the media, for example) that tone has become condescending and judgmental toward traditional Christian perspectives, and all the more stridently persecutorial against those who stand up and make their convictions heard.

I believe this is lost on the general public, but the worst of it is, many Christians are oblivious to it as well. As I have observed this sad reality, my concern has grown for the Christian church and the response of its people to the changes in the world around them. Millions of Protestant and Catholic and Orthodox men and women are not resisting the onslaught of cultural change. The world's cancer is slowly and inexorably undermining the outlook and worldview of all segments of Christendom.

Some time ago my friend Joseph Dindinger alerted me to the book *The Benedict Option*, and another friend encouraged me to read its sequel, *Live Not by Lies*. Both these books, as you will see, were pivotal in my own evolving response to the times. I am also deeply appreciative to our friend Nick Harrison, mentioned in the dedication, for his influential role in the genesis of this book.

Eventually I realized it was time for me also to speak out and, in Martin Luther's immortal words, be bold to say, "Here I stand."

Our country is at a crossroads. To be faithful to my convictions, both as a Christian and an American, I offer this one man's perspective of the divide that comprises this national crossroads. It is a divide not between conservative and liberal (I hope I am both). It is not a divide between looking forward or looking back (I hope I am capable of both). Neither is it a divide between modernism and traditionalism (I hope I am able to see the benefits of both). Nor is it a divide between Democrat or Republican (I am neither). The debate is not between different systems of faith (I have never been a Christian legalist and am enthusiastically aware that *all* men and women have much to teach me).

It is a divide between the virtue and what I call the "unvirtue" of a nation and its people.

The subtitle may cause a little confusion but is used intentionally. Sometimes I may refer to the *coming* ideological war and at other times speak of that war as *already* upon us. Both statements are true. World War II opened in September of 1939 with a protracted period when nothing much happened. It was called the "Phony War." Germany had invaded Poland, and England had declared war on Germany, but then for eight months neither side did anything further of consequence. The *real* war was yet to come.

That is exactly the situation in which we find ourselves. Progressivism has declared war on its adversaries. Nor would anyone call it a phony war. It's real enough. But compared to what is coming, it may be, "We ain't seen nothing yet." We are *in* the ideological war, and it will get worse.

Despite surface appearances, I do not write this primarily as a *political* book. I realize this may be misunderstood as we go along because political issues will necessarily come into it. Yet if anyone interprets what follows as a political treatise, they will miss the underlying message.

The paramount theme addresses these questions: How is the church, and how are individual Christians meeting the changes of our time? What ought to be Christendom's response to a culture drifting ever further from America's historic moorings? Are Catholic and Protestant and Orthodox men and women whose faith and church lives are important to them intended to walk a *different* path than those in the general culture who profess no faith? Or is it fine to *go along* passively with the same cultural values the world is seeking to impose on everyone?

My objective is to inquire what kind of people serious Christians are called to be. Hopefully we can give intelligent and prayerful thought to our responses to changes that are coming to the world with startling forcefulness but have been met with equally astonishing complacency by a public seemingly asleep to their implications.

These changes demand a response. Silence, neutrality, and docile compliance will not be an option much longer.

– Part 1 –
Virtues and Unvirtues

1

GOODNESS
the unvirtue: evil

There is no swifter route to the corruption of thought
than through the corruption of language.
— George Orwell

Many terms in common use today have lost their traditional meaning. If these changes in definition—or even *perceived* meaning—help increase clarity, it's generally a good thing. If they hinder clarity and obscure meaning, these changes are *un*helpful.

Words and Meanings

Words like *traditional* and *progressive*, *liberal* and *conservative* are taking on new and highly charged nuances that would not have occurred to those hearing them during the 1950s or earlier. A more perfect example could not exist than the word *gay*. Not only has its meaning shifted entirely; it has become such a culturally loaded word it is now impossible to use "gay" in its former and traditional sense. The new meaning has obliterated the old definition and rendered it obsolete.

Many words are coming under scrutiny in this rush to change what everything means: *man, woman, gender, sex, black, white, legal, illegal, criminal, binary, right, wrong, good, bad.* It's hard to keep up. You never know when you might use a term another considers offensive because it doesn't conform to the new meaning. You might never even have heard of the new meaning! Yet you might give offence and be completely in the dark as to why.

9

This trend is so important to begin any discussion on any topic that the great linguist and logician C. S. Lewis clarified this very thing in the preface to his classic *Mere Christianity.* He was writing in 1952, and his insight is as forceful today as it was then. His point was straightforward: if words are expanded so far beyond their original intent, and made so inclusive as to mean anything anyone wants them to mean, then they lose meaning altogether. They become useless words.

> The word *gentleman* originally meant something recognisable; one who had a coat of arms and some landed property. When you called someone "a gentleman" you were not paying him a compliment, but merely stating a fact. If you said he was not "a gentleman" you were not insulting him, but giving information. There was no contradiction in saying that John was a liar and a gentleman; . . . But then there came people who said— so rightly, charitably, spiritually, sensitively, so anything but usefully—"Ah, but surely the important thing about a gentleman is not the coat of arms and the land, but the behaviour? Surely he is a true gentleman who behaves as a gentleman should?" . . . They meant well. To be honourable and courteous and brave is of course a far better thing than to have a coat of arms. But it is not the same thing. Worse still, it is not a thing everyone will agree about. . . . When a word ceases to be a term of description . . . it no longer tells you facts about the object: it only tells you about the speaker's attitude to that object. . . . A *gentleman* . . . means hardly more than a man whom the speaker likes. As a result, *gentleman* is now a useless word. . . .
>
> Now if once we allow people to start . . . refining, or as they might say "deepening," the sense of the word *Christian*, it too will speedily become a useless word. In

the first place, Christians themselves will never be able to apply it to anyone. . . . As for the unbelievers, they will no doubt cheerfully use the word in the refined sense. It will become in their mouths simply a term of praise. In calling anyone a Christian they will mean that they think him a good man. But that way of using the word will be no enrichment of the language, for we already have the word *good*. Meanwhile, the word *Christian* will have been spoiled for any really useful purpose it might have served.[1]

Lewis's *Studies in Words,* published years later, was entirely devoted to word changes. In it Lewis used the word *verbicide*, which technically means deliberately distorting a word's meaning, to carry more lethal consequence. "Verbicide," he wrote, "the murder of a word, happens in many ways. . . . [T]he greatest cause of verbicide is the fact that most people are obviously far more anxious to express their approval and disapproval of things than to describe them. Hence the tendency of words to become less descriptive and more evaluative . . . and to end up being purely evaluative—useless synonyms for *good* or for *bad*."[2]

Do Changes in Meaning Blur or Enhance Clarity?

All this is so much a part of our lives that it goes without saying. Everyone reading these words will have heard the word *Christian* used to mean "a nice person" and will probably have also heard someone take offense at it being said of someone else, that he or she is *not* a Christian, as if it were an insult rather than a statement of fact. What Lewis predicted has indeed come to pass. For Christians themselves, the word still holds deep and personal meaning. In the general culture, however, it is even worse than Lewis imagined. Not only is the word *Christian* useless; it has ceased to be a word synonymous with *good* at all. For many, it has become a term of derision and disparagement, synonymous with bigotry, narrow-mindedness, and judgmentalism. The actual meaning of the word, for such critics, has flipped upside-down.

Many terms in today's culture are suffering the same fate. Everything is being redefined before our eyes. And not for the better—not, in Lewis's terminology, toward *usefulness*. This wholesale redefining of terms is neither producing clarity nor an increase of truth but, rather, confusion and a blurring of truth. A simple term like *gender*—which has a specific linguistic definition* but which modernism has co-opted in order to expand the meaning of biological birth sex—if you take seriously some of the more far-reaching definitions being put forward, now has, at last count (though this changes even as I write) as many as seventy-two different nuanced meanings.† Whether this is a good or a bad thing is in the eye of the beholder. But we can probably all agree it is a development that has muddled not illuminated truth. *Truth* itself is one of the terms on the endangered list.

The term *American* is another concept on its way toward uselessness along with *gentleman, Christian, gender, good*, and *truth*. It used to mean something very specific. However, it is not hard to imagine overhearing the following conversation:

"I'm an American."
"Are you a U.S. citizen?
"No."
"Were you born in the U.S.?"

---

* This meaning of the word is often lost to native English speakers and is most notable in languages such as Spanish and German, which identify nouns as either masculine, feminine, or neuter.

† Though the seventy-two options may sound far-fetched, the options on some driver's license and passport application are no less illogical to common sense. "Personal identification:

Female, as biologically born	Male identifying as female without surgery
Male, as biologically born	Male identifying as female with surgical conversion
Female identifying as male without surgery	Bi-sexual, no orientation specified
	Other, please specify (optional):_____
Female identifying as male with surgical conversion	_____
	None of the above."

"No."
"Are your parents U.S. citizens?"
"No."
"Do you speak English?"
"A little."
"Did you immigrate to the U.S. legally?"
"No."
"Have you passed the citizenship requirements?"
"No. But I'm an American."

Nor is it unlikely, if one were to inadvertently cross some invisible lines of political correctness, that he or she might be summarily rebuked, "How can you say such a thing—*you're* no American!"

American is on its way to becoming a term that can mean an individual someone thinks ought to be able to live in this country with no strings of legality or citizenship or language or birth or parentage or anything else attached.

What Is Good?

As shrewd as were his observations, C. S. Lewis fell short of predicting how far this trend of word-uselessness would go, and what would be its devastating results for understanding truth. His reference to the word *good* is a case in point. Not only is *good* no longer synonymous with *Christian*; little meaning is left in the word at all. Exactly as he said, *good* simply means whatever someone likes. Conservatives call one thing good, progressives call the opposite good. A "good" person is a value judgment, meaning little more, as Lewis says, than a person "whom the speaker likes." A juvenile delinquent who shoots a shopkeeper is defended by parents and friends and teachers: "He just fell in with the wrong crowd, but he's really a good kid."

All this leads us to the point, obvious by now, that *virtue* is a word exactly like *good* and all these others. It can mean anything anyone wants it to. How can we engage in a discussion of "endangered" virtues when the word itself is endangered?

It may be a challenge. But I am optimistic in thinking that neither goodness nor virtue are altogether dead yet. I hope we can come to a meeting of the minds sufficiently to engage in an intelligent and rational discussion about what virtue is and what are some of its implications in our lives. Such a meeting of the minds in today's volatile climate may be difficult. But at least I can clarify how I am using the words I will employ in this book. Hopefully my definitions can provide a basis, as I say, for intelligent and rational dialog. You may use some of the terms differently. At least you will know how I am using them for this discussion of virtue.

2

Virtue
the unvirtue: vice

The happiness of your life depends upon the quality of your thoughts: therefore, guard accordingly, and take care that you entertain no notions unsuitable to virtue.
— Marcus Aurelius

As I began this chapter, out of curiosity I entered "virtue" in my computer's thesaurus. Several of the definitions focused on the words *good* or *goodness*. I agree completely with that perspective. If virtue is to mean anything, it must certainly be synonymous with goodness. If *goodness*, however, no longer has meaning to modern ears, how does that help us understand *virtue*? Will the next step be saying the teen who shot the convenience store clerk is a young man of virtue because he's a "good kid"?

If this discussion is to get off the ground, a more potent, accurate, vigorous, and useful definition is necessary. Mere *goodness*, as much as that perhaps *ought* to mean, isn't enough.

Virtue and Vice

Webster's 1828 dictionary drives us back to a time when words *meant* what they meant. It gets us much closer to the core substance of *virtue*: "Strength . . . . Bravery; valor. . . . Moral goodness; the practice of moral duties and the abstaining from vice, or a conformity of life and conversation to the moral law. . . . A particular moral excellence. . . . Acting power . . . . Excellence; or that which constitutes value and merit. . . . Efficacy; power. . . ."[1]

15

This is but a brief overview. But it certainly adds powerful specificity to the idea of virtue beyond fuzzy notions of goodness. It sweeps up into it the strength and courage to *be* good, to *choose* to be good, to resist urges and temptations toward wrong, to stand with valor for moral excellence. Virtue implies no passive goodness but active, dynamic, muscular goodness.

Now it might be said the teen holding the gun was exhibiting bravery, even power. But that is hardly enough. Did he *choose* goodness? Did he *resist* the temptation to do wrong? Was he brave enough to choose right over wrong? The "bravery" of virtue does not exist in a vacuum. There is also such a thing as *moral law* to be considered. How does that young man's virtue and character hold up when standing before the mirror of moral law? By the reflection of that mirror, can he still be called a *good* kid?

Notice something else embedded in the above definition: "abstaining from vice."

Virtue has an opposite. This is a more significant truth than may at first be apparent. Though my computer's thesaurus lists "antonyms" along with definitions, and presumably the word *antonym* is still a concept taught in high school English, in practice few antonyms are left in today's modern culture. The very idea of antonyms has become an imaginary cultural phantom. If *good* can mean anything you want, so can *bad*. Is something against the law? Never mind, if you're underprivileged and have a good reason, we won't call it breaking the law. We won't call what you did "bad."

Good and *evil* used to be clearly understood opposites. Not anymore. Evil, like good, is in the eye of the beholder. The teen is let off with a slap on the wrist. He's a "good kid" after all.

A concept like "vice," therefore, is also endangered. We're not allowed to call anything "wrong" or "bad" or "sinful" or "corrupt" or "illegal" anymore. Vice, in a traditional sense, no longer exists.*

---

* This actually isn't 100 percent the case. That's why the caveat "in the traditional sense." Progressivism still acknowledges *evil* and *vice* just as it does *goodness* and *virtue*. But they are so redefined by its convoluted matrix of new definitions that the Webster definitions become nonsense in progressivism's ears. In that woke matrix of new meanings, those

Therefore, the statement in the definition above that virtue means "abstaining from vice" may be meaningless to modern ears. But if we're trying to understand virtue in a true, meaningful, and useful sense, that statement is of enormous import.

Antonyms exist.

Virtue has an opposite, an *unvirtue*. That opposite is vice: "a spot or defect; a fault; a blemish. . . . In ethics, any voluntary action or course of conduct which deviates from the rules of moral rectitude, or from the plain rules of propriety; any moral unfitness of conduct, either from defect of duty, or from the transgression of known principles of rectitude. . . . Depravity or corruption of manners. . . ."[2]

A Culture without Antonyms

Modernity does not hold to the truth of moral or virtue-opposites because it does not believe right and wrong exist. It does not believe that bad is the opposite of good, that wrong is the opposite of right, that sin is the opposite of righteousness, that illegality is the opposite of legality. *Moral law, moral excellence, moral unfitness of conduct, known principles of rectitude*—these fundamental truths of virtue and vice have lost all meaning in modernity's lexicon of values. It may seem that we have become a culture without antonyms.

But these terms have not lost meaning to me, nor to many who still value virtue in the traditional sense.

There *are* unvirtues as surely as there are virtues. Unvirtues deviate from "moral rectitude" or from "the plain rules of propriety." They transgress "known principles of rectitude."

---

holding to Christian values and beliefs and definitions of right and wrong, and Americans who revere the country's roots, are actually unvirtuous, wrong, and some would go so far as to call it "evil" to hold those beliefs. Meanwhile, those who judge, condemn, and ostracize those same Christians are considered right and virtuous for doing so. Crossing the border illegally is a *good* thing in progressivism's eyes; standing for the rule of law in that instance is a *bad* thing.

To the seeker after meaningful *virtue*, those known principles of ethics, morality, and rectitude are among the anchoring foundation stones of truth.*

As we progress, we will widen the idea of virtue to encompass many qualities of attitude and behavior that, to use our title phrase, are endangered in the modern culture of the United States of America in the decade of the 2020s. To discuss them, it will be imperative also to discuss their opposites. This may be a hurdle too high for those who no longer hold to the concept of antonyms, who do not believe that such a thing as unvirtue even exists.

Nonetheless, this book is based on a premise that should be made as clear as can be stated:

Antonyms exist.

There are opposites in the world.

Virtue and *unvirtue* are not compatible.

The demarcation between opposites, however, does not need to be a line of argument, hostility, or anger. Our common and universal humanity binds us together in a unity far deeper than our differences of perspective on any issue, whether religious, political, racial, or cultural. That it does often lead to anger and hostility is but another example of unvirtue sowing its poison among us.

---

* A brief linguistic clarification may be worth mentioning. *Vice*, as used in this definition, primarily speaks of actions—doing wrong things, making wrong moral choices. My use of the word *virtue*, on the other hand, emerges out of the people we *are* more than in what we *do*. Virtue speaks of *character*. Of course a virtuous character leads to virtuous actions and attitudes. But to be technically accurate, the parallel terms should be something like virtue vs. vicefulness. That is obviously cumbersome, so I will let words stand as I have them.

3

ABSOLUTES
the unvirtue: relativism

The American elite is almost beyond redemption. . . . Moral relativism has set in
so deeply that the gilded classes have become incapable of discerning
right from wrong. Everything can be explained away, especially by journalists.
Life is one great moral mush—sophistry washed down with Chardonnay.
The ordinary citizens, thank goodness, still adhere to absolutes.

— Charles Dickens

Francis Schaeffer (1912–84) was arguably the twentieth century's most profound Christian thinker, theologian, and apologist.
Though Lewis devotees may squawk, no disclaimer is needed such as
"with apologies to C. S. Lewis," for he needs none. The men wrote on
different themes and to different audiences. Schaeffer was a philosopher, historian, and theologian; Lewis a populist. Together they did
more to advance the logical underpinnings of Christian truth than
any recent tandem of writers one can think of. Nor are we compelled
to rank them at all. Both stand in the hall of fame of my personal
mentors' gallery, their books next to me every day as I write.

Antithesis—The Basis for Understanding Truth

Schaeffer's corpus of work, though not so widely known as Lewis's,
is equally vast and probably even more far reaching. To summarize it
in any sense, not to mention briefly, is impossible. I will but abridge
what may be its most important aspect by saying that Schaeffer illuminated the loss of absolutist thinking that was inundating modern

culture. He did so by tracing the abandonment of absolutes historically in diverse fields—philosophy, theology, music, art, and science. To his analysis he added shrewd insights into the impact of this change on the general culture. Upon the basis of antithesis, he showed that modern young people are being taught to think according to a relativistic paradigm completely at odds with that by which people have thought at any previous time in history.

That new foundation of thought is built on the premise that there are no opposites in the arena of truth that inform knowledge, understanding, and experience and are meant to regulate personal choice. Accordingly, today truth is relative not absolute. The results of this shift toward relativism are devastating to the understanding of spiritual principles anchored in absolutist truth and to an understanding of everything history has to teach us.

While much of Schaeffer's writing is dense and abstruse, he opened his first and perhaps most important work, *The God Who Is There,* clearly setting out the themes that undergirded his subsequent twenty books—themes that essentially (though obviously oversimplified) define his legacy.

> The present chasm between the generations has been brought about almost entirely by a change in the concept of truth. . . . *[M]*en and women are being fundamentally affected by the new way of looking at truth, . . . Before . . . everyone would have been working on much the same presuppositions. . . . The basic one was that there really are such things as absolutes. . . . Therefore, because they accepted . . . absolutes, though men might disagree as to what these were, nevertheless they could reason together on the classical basis of antithesis. So if anything was true, the opposite was false. In morality, if one thing was right, its opposite was wrong. This little formula, "If you have A, it is not non-A" is the first move in classical logic. . . . Thus it was still possible to discuss what was right and wrong, what was true and false.[1]

Schaeffer went on to detail how "the flood-waters of secular thought," as he described it, affect every one of us and almost every conversation we engage in. The remarkable thing is, these words were written more than fifty years ago. To call them prophetic is an under-statement. The passage of the decades has proved Francis Schaeffer a far more astute prophet of the future than Hal Lindsey, whose *The Late Great Planet Earth* was published in 1967, a year before Schaeffer's first book. It is now Schaeffer's words that have become the reality of life on planet Earth as we approach the second quarter of the third millennium, not Lindsey's.

A Flood of New Useless Words

It is no longer that people differ about what truth is or differ on what constitutes right and wrong. Modern secular men and women are such thorough relativists that they no longer believe right and wrong, good and bad, and virtue and unvirtue exist at all. Those are abso-lutist words. For the modernist, they have no meaning. There is no *absolute* truth. Right, wrong, good, bad, truth, and virtue are *relative*. They are different for everyone. They mean whatever you want them to mean.

This difference is huge. We mustn't miss the full scope of it. It's far more than one person saying, "I believe God exists," and another saying, "I don't believe God exists." That is a classic A vs. non-A dif-ference—what Schaeffer called *antithesis* thinking. There have always been believers and atheists, and they understood each other well enough. They disagreed, but they understood each other.

That has entirely changed. The modernist would say, for the Christian, that God really and truly *does* exist, and for the atheist, that God really and truly does *not* exist. Not pretend exist—*really* exists and *really* doesn't exist.

The illogic is profound. But this is how modern children, high school students, and young college men and women are all being taught to think. This paradigm has been the standard for well over two generations now, such that essentially the entire modern culture from ages 0 to 50 or 60 thinks about everything according to this falsehood.

This is what makes dialog about anything—religion, politics, law, immigration, sex, marriage, anything and everything—difficult. There are no rules, no boundaries to definitions. Even definitions themselves have little meaning. Everyone makes up their own.

If you say, "This is true," the modern secularist replies, "If that is true for you, I'm happy for you. But the opposite is true for me." And they really mean it. They are incapable of grasping the logical absurdity of what they say. They actually believe two opposing and mutually exclusive things can both be true. The title of Schaeffer's companion volume, published almost simultaneously with *The God Who Is There*, entitled *Escape from Reason,* is brilliantly prophetic.

The more *reason* you try to bring to the table, the more hopeless the exchange becomes. Because as Schaeffer said, classic logic no longer applies. Logic as well as antithetical thinking has been thrown out the window.

As modernism defines *truth*, not merely two opposite ideas but seventeen opposing ideas can *all* be true. As it defines *right,* two opposite actions or seventeen different actions can *all* be right. The rules of critical thinking have shifted on their axis.

Yet in the world of relativism, it all makes perfect sense.

Lewis was equally prophetic with his analysis of the trend toward useless words. For the secularist whose worldview is rooted in relativism, *truth* and *falsehood*, *right* and *wrong*, *goodness* and *virtue* are all now useless words.

The underlying thesis of this book—that *virtues* and *unvirtues* exist; they are real and opposites—for the modernist will be a nonsensical premise. As Schaeffer imagined the response to the statement, "Be a good girl," I might imagine the response of many to the notion of virtues and unvirtues as opposites: "The blank look you might receive would not mean that your standards had been rejected but that your message was meaningless."[2]

Into this relativistic milieu in which we find ourselves, then, this discussion will proceed with the central idea of this chapter: that *recognition of absolutes* is itself a virtue. It is vital for the future of this country that *virtue* and *absolutes* not become useless words. It is virtuous to order one's life by logic, reason, and absolutes as they are understood in the classical sense.

It is a virtue to recognize:

- there is such a thing as truth and falsehood;
- they are not the same;
- right and wrong exist;
- they are not the same;
- good and evil exist;
- they are not the same;
- virtue and vice exist;
- they are not the same;
- some ideas and lifestyles and habits and attitudes are virtuous according to real standards; and
- some ideas and lifestyles and habits and attitudes are *not* virtuous and do *not* represent truth by those same standards.

The underlying foundation is straightforward enough: *A and non-A are opposites. Antonyms in life exist. Virtue and unvirtue are not compatible.*

In the same way that Jesus said in Mark 4:13, "Do you not understand this parable? How then will you understand all the parables?" we might say, "If you do not understand this foundational principle, how will you understand all the principles of truth." Or specific to our purpose for this discussion, "If you do not recognize absolutes, how will you understand virtue?"

4

COMMON SENSE
the unvirtue: illogic

Republics are created by the virtue, public spirit, and intelligence
of the citizens. They fall, when the wise are banished from the
public councils, because they dare to be honest, and the profligate
are rewarded, because they flatter the people, in order to betray them.

— Joseph Story*

The trouble with absolutes is, they come in all sizes and shapes. Not all absolutes are created equal. Some are more "absolute" than others.

Some rise to the level of truth, some of mere fact. Many things in life *are* indeed relative. Two plus two equals four is an absolute fact. A relativist cannot say, "But for *me*, two plus two equals five." The laws of mathematics are absolute.†

That I drive a blue car, however, might be considered an absolute fact. The car in our garage *is* blue, not red. But it is an insignificant absolute of little importance to anyone else. It may be a *fact*, but it is not a *law* such as those that regulate mathematics. Furthermore, it is subject to individual choice, which mathematics is not. Though our car being blue may be incontrovertible, buying that car was a relative choice. What may have been the right choice for me may not be the

---

* Joseph Story was a justice of the Supreme Court of the United States from 1812 to 1845. As a prolific author of legal treatises, he is considered one of the most renowned constitutional scholars in American history.

† Incredibly, extreme relativists are challenging even the absolutes of such simple mathematics as 2 + 2 = 4.

right choice for you. Those are *relative* decisions. Neither one of us can elevate our relative decisions and turn them into absolutes, saying it is *right* by a universal standard to drive a blue or red or gray car, and that people who make a different choice are *wrong*. In such a case, there exists a fluid intermingling of choices (which are relative) and solid facts (which in a limited sense might be considered absolutes).

Other factors come into it as well. All of us driving cars of different color according to our *relative* choices are yet bound by the universal and *absolute* laws of the road. We may not hurt anyone by driving sixty-two miles per hour when the speed limit is sixty. We may not be ticketed, and everybody may do it. But it is nevertheless against the law. That is an absolute. The law is clear and unbending. The law is absolute whether we choose to obey it or not.

The Continuum of Importance

Yet there is a continuum of importance within the absoluteness of the law. Driving 115 miles per hour is *more* against the law. It is a greater violation and will have more serious consequences than driving sixty-two. That's what is meant by saying that all absolutes are not the same.

This is not relativism; it is common-sense elasticity. A spectrum of importance and consequence exists within both relativism and absolutism, which a mature and open-minded outlook enables us clearly to distinguish. We have to think and evaluate truth with common sense, not illogic.

One may say, "If you believe you should obey the law and not go above sixty, that may be right for you. But I do not consider it wrong unless I exceed the speed limit by more than fifteen miles per hour."

He may make that choice and drive any speed he chooses, but it's still breaking the law. He is violating an absolute law even though he is using relativistic reasoning to do so.*

---

* Even here, there are loopholes. Exceptions can be found for *all* these points if one wants to dissect them to pieces. We might raise the distinction between "written law" and "applied law"—jaywalking, for example, or going a few miles per hour over the speed

Making a relative choice in responding to the law does not make that absolute nonexistent. The law is still there. Relativism doesn't make absolutes go away even for those who pretend it is so. The parallel with moral law is not difficult to see.

There are absolutes, but we have freedom to make individual and relative choices in response to those absolutes. It's called free will. Absolutes will always function in complex interplay with free will.

The Shifting Goal Posts of Modernism

In our time, relativism is justified, as above, by saying that absolutes don't exist, thus removing right and wrong from the moral equation. All this does, however, is move the absolutist goalposts. The absolutes still exist. But those who ignore them are exercising their relative free will to pretend they can move the absolutes so far out of sight that they feel comfortable ignoring them. Saying, "I don't consider it wrong to go fifteen miles per hour above the speed limit," doesn't eliminate the law.

Many quandaries of morality, ethics, legality, and virtue can be explained in precisely this way. In some respects, this form of relativism has existed throughout history. People have always broken laws. What has changed in our time is, when you remind the relativist of the law, you will be condemned as narrow-minded, behind the times,

---

limit when no officer will ticket you for it. However, we're not trying to put forward a thorough dissertation on absolutism and relativism, or what we might also call objectivity and subjectivity, but to establish certain basic principles that will allow thinking men and women to see the difference in how people think and respond to ideas. In this case, the "absolute" of the speed limit is different than the "absolute" laws of mathematics. Speed limits are man-made and thus subject to a certain relativism as well (different states have different speed limits). The laws of mathematics are determined by the nature of the universe itself. (Though even this might be quibbled with, in that Newton and Einstein were men too, who codified many of the laws of mathematics.) Therefore it might be said, and many do say it, "That's a man-made law, and I do not recognize its validity." This is especially an argument made by secularists regarding moral and spiritual laws. For now, however, hopefully we do not need to be completely sidetracked with such analytical nitpicking. We will continue to use the analogy of the speed limit as an example (imperfect as it may be) of an absolute that impacts us all every day but which people respond to differently in a relative and individual manner.

hypocritical, and judgmental. It has become bigoted and ignorant to point out that words have meaning (including absolute, law, morality, ethics, right, wrong, good, bad). There is no end to the disparaging attacks made against one who raises the reminder that certain speed limits of behavior still exist even if people choose to ignore them.

Nowhere is pretending speed limits no longer exist more destructive to the ethical and spiritual underpinnings of individual and national character than in the moral relativism that has so infected our culture it is now almost completely normalized.

Legalism and License

Recognizing the absolutes inherent in certain moral, historical, ethical, and spiritual speed limits and goalposts does not justify legalism anymore than moving the goalposts and ignoring the speed limits justifies license. Nuance and common sense remain important factors, not only for constructive dialog but in contributing to personal maturity and the flourishing of wisdom and personal wholeness. That's why common sense is one of life's pivotal virtues. Without common sense, we can't think clearly and logically.

Progressivist legalism is one of the best kept, dirty little secrets of our time. Legalism is equally destructive to open-mindedness and growth in the fundamentalist Christian *and* in the secular modernist. Both can be legalists. They are just legalistic about their own (differing) perspectives about where the goalposts should stand. The secularist who angrily condemns the fundamentalist for his legalism about morals is equally legalistic about his *license* in ignoring the moral goalposts altogether. Progressives who ignore their own judgmental legalisms are fooling no one but themselves.

Navigating the fluid continuum between these twin legalisms, and understanding the complexities involved in the positions of the goalposts on opposite sides of the field, requires wisdom, objectivity, humility—and common sense.

These conundrums are especially difficult when objectively trying to discuss moral and ethical absolutes. The goalposts are difficult to define. They're not like mathematical laws that everyone agrees upon. We're engaged in a contest of ideas where entirely different rulebooks govern how people think and behave on opposite sides of the fifty-yard line. The two opposite goalposts extend down into the soils of entirely different worldviews.

Even Absolutes Are Relative

The determination of what constitutes absolutes is itself relative. Some absolutes are not *absolutely* "absolute." A Christian may say abortion is an absolute wrong. A secular relativist may say, "But I do not consider it wrong." And that will be a true statement.

Which of the two individuals is right? Is abortion absolute or relative? It can't be both. If it is an absolute, the relativist is wrong. If it is a relative choice, the absolutist is wrong.

Many moral absolutes are rooted in religious mores, teachings, traditions, and taboos—abortion, foul language, homosexuality, adultery, sex outside marriage, same-sex marriage, and many others we could name. Most of these, however, are no longer viewed as absolutes (right or wrong) culturally. They are even being normalized in the church. But religious and nonreligious men and women alike would have been revolted by these practices a hundred years ago as violations of moral law, common decency, and known standards of right and wrong. They have now drifted over the fence and are considered by most of the culture perfectly acceptable.

Other absolutes, though perhaps reflected in spiritual teachings, overreach cultural and societal differences. The Ten Commandments are not obsolete yet. Stealing, lying, killing, adultery, and so on span most religions and societies. Many secularists would probably likewise agree that honor of one's parents is generally healthy and covetousness is generally not.

Yet even universal standards have nuanced differences. What role does *motive* play in determining right or wrong? There may also be distinctions of judgment depending on circumstance. Is stealing to feed a starving child wrong? Is lying for the right motive wrong? Is killing to prevent the murder of an innocent wrong? How far do circumstances justify breaking a moral or ethical law?

In other words, how much do we excuse on the basis of motive? Is war justified for good motives? (Though who defines "good" in a relativistic world?) The Hitler conundrum then rears its head: How many otherwise ethical standards are allowed to be broken to combat evil? With *good* now a relatively interpreted idea, who arbitrates what constitutes a good motive, a righteous conflict, a justifiable war, Hitler or Churchill? Standing face to face in front of the former, would murder itself have been justified?

5

LOVE OF TRUTH
the unvirtue: love of opinion

First we overlook evil. Then we permit evil. Then we legalize evil.
Then we promote evil. Then we celebrate evil.
Then we persecute those who still call it evil.
— Father Dwight Longenecker

The deeper we probe into morality and ethics, the more complex and elusive become absolute absolutes. Terminology is as important as motive. What is *meant* by the words we use? Who decides good from evil?

The universe is *big* says the astronomer. On its face, it seems to be an absolute no one can argue with. No one, perhaps, except the quantum physicist or molecular biologist whose world deals with the infinitesimally *small* universe of molecules, atoms, and subatomic particles. Those involved in these three disciplines may all define what they mean by "universe" differently.

Francis Schaeffer again set up the issues of language, meaning, and reality with clarity:

> The problem . . . is not only in language but in reality . . . .
> This . . . is most easily understood in the area of morals. If
> there is no absolute moral standard, then one cannot say
> in a final sense that anything is right or wrong. By *absolute*,
> we mean that which always applies, that which provides
> a final or ultimate standard. There must be an absolute if
> there are to be *morals*, and there must be an absolute if

31

there are to be real *values*. If there is no absolute beyond man's ideas, then there is no final appeal to judge between individuals and groups whose moral judgments conflict. We are merely left with conflicting opinions.

But it is not only that we need absolutes in morals and values; we need absolutes if our existence is to have *meaning*—my existence, your existence, Man's existence. Even more profoundly, we must have absolutes if we are to have a solid epistemology (a theory of knowing—how we know, or how we know we know). How can we be sure that what we think we know of the world outside ourselves really corresponds to what is there . . . unless there is an absolute these things are lost to us: morals, values, the meaning of existence (including the meaning of man), and a basis for knowing.[1]

Schaeffer wrote those words more than four decades ago. As modernity's headlong race to abolish absolutes has accelerated, that might as well be a century. On the mark as his words are, the language of relativism has almost entirely deteriorated modernity's capacity to understand, much less talk about truth. What is meant by right and wrong is now blurred into near hopelessness. The playing field and its goalposts are almost unrecognizable from Schaeffer's time.

The overriding question facing us *today* is far more complex. How do we determine which issues are absolute, implying a value judgment if violated, and which are relative, with no value judgment no matter what the individual choice? Schaeffer might have asked the same thing. But the divide represented by that question is so much wider now it is virtually impossible to talk about *truth* in an objective way when the *absolutist/objective* perspective of truth and the *relativistic/subjective* view are worlds apart. They are no longer even playing on the same field. They are not only playing their half of the game each on their own side of the fifty-yard line but in two different stadiums across town.

No wonder we have a hard time communicating!

The Quagmire of Morality and Ethics

An equally important question is, How do love of truth and personal opinion intermingle? Are all *my* opinions true and yours are not? Obviously that cannot be. Yet functionally and conversationally that is how most of us communicate.

Stepping back from that obvious short-sightedness then, how can I determine which of my opinions may in fact be untrue and should be discarded? Do I have courage to ask where truth may *not* reside in some of my opinions?

We obviously live in a time when much in the world and in our personal lives is viewed as *relative* or *subjective* by those of a progressive outlook, while people of more traditional perspective view more aspects of life and the world through a lens of *absolutes* or *objectivity*. But where are *both* sides—traditionalism and progressivism—infected with opinions that are not true? And who's to adjudicate that controversial determination?

I hope it is clear we're not trying to resolve every specific into a right vs. wrong, absolutism vs. relativism grid. It *is* important, however, to understand certain general overarching principles that explain how men and women of divergent worldviews think and arrive at the conclusions regulating their attitudes, outlook, and behavior.

The High Plane of Transcendent Truth

The somewhat clunky intellectual term *epistemic virtue* is used to denote the ability to objectively perceive truth above and independent of one's own opinions and biases.

Are the traditionalist and the secularist both "epistemically virtuous" thinkers? Are they able to lay aside their preconceptions and rise above the low realm of opinion, stepping up to evaluate truth on the high level of objectivity?

Is the traditionalist able to say, "It may be my religion that has taught me abortion is an absolute wrong, but perhaps that is an opinionated bias of my religion"?

Is the secularist able to say, "It may be the culture in which I am immersed that has taught me abortion is a decision of relative individual choice, but perhaps that is an opinionated bias I have wrongly absorbed from the culture"?

In this process, there come times when open-minded humility, at the end of much sincere and honest reflection, will conclude, "My belief *does* represent high truth. It is *not* motivated by indoctrination, opinion, or cultural bias. I believe what I believe, and I believe I have arrived at that perspective objectively."

Let us not be *too* hasty to excuse ourselves from bias. Yet some perspectives *do* indeed reflect truth. Others do not. It *is* possible to objectively assert that certain things truly violate standards of absolute truth, right and wrong.

Who among us, as Schaeffer termed it, are "people with more understanding" who are willing to give "careful consideration of what world-view is true?" Who among us is able to lay aside bias, demonstrating the maturity and wisdom to seek truth that transcends opinion, raising himself or herself—by humility and open-mindedness—up into the region of high truth where the worth and sanctity of life is inviolate?

How many other transcendent truths exist on that lofty plane that can only be apprehended by escaping the suffocating fog of opinion, cultural drift, religious doctrine, conformity, and intellectual apathy?

Where do we lay hold of life's transcendent truths?

Differing Worldviews

In the end it essentially comes down to what people believe. Opening his landmark book, *How Should We Then Live?*, already quoted, written toward the end of his writing life as a fitting bookend to *The God Who Is There,* Francis Schaeffer summarized:

> People are unique in the inner life of the mind—what they are in their thought-world determines how they act. This is true of their value systems . . . . It is true of their

corporate actions, such as political decisions, and it is true of their personal lives. . . .

People have presuppositions, and they will live more consistently on the basis of these presuppositions than even they themselves may realize. By *presuppositions* we mean the basic way an individual looks at life, his basic world-view, the grid through which he sees the world. Presuppositions rest upon that which a person considers to be the truth of what exists. People's presuppositions lay a grid for all they bring forth into the external world. Their presuppositions also provide the basis for their values and therefore the basis for their decisions. . . .

Most people catch their presuppositions from their family and surrounding society the way a child catches measles. But people with more understanding realize that their presuppositions should be chosen after a careful consideration of what world-view is true. When all is done, when all the alternatives have been explored . . . although world-views have many variations, there are not many basic world-views or basic presuppositions.[2]

In other words, few worldviews lead out of the confusing and contradictory mists of relativism up to the high plane of transcendent truth. It may take great courage for some—religious traditionalist and secular progressive alike—to lay aside their ill-conceived presuppositions and embark on the inner quest for a worldview rooted in transcendent truth, not transitory opinion, doctrinal jargon, or cultural indoctrination.

The Practicality of the Absolute-Relativist Divide

These chapters on how absolutist and relativist thinking impacts how we view the world may have seemed at first read to be largely theoretical and philosophical. If such was your takeaway, I encourage you to wait two or three days and read them again. Upon further review, you may discover this one of the most practical sections of the book. You may then find this discussion of absolutes and relativism, common sense and illogic, truth and opinion helpful in bringing clarity to many of the unthinkably bewildering behaviors, practices, and viewpoints we all observe and hear expressed around us every day.

The principles of these chapters explain why words that have had clear meanings for thousands of years (marriage, gender, man, woman, family, fidelity, parenthood, justice, equality, violence, discrimination) are suddenly being redefined in the most bizarre and illogical ways—and no one objects.

The principles of these chapters explain our immigration crisis and why rules, standards, borders, and the former canons constituting nationhood and citizenship are no longer defined and regulated by the laws of the land—and no one on the left objects.

These principles explain why it is now considered principled, even virtuous, for certain groups in our society to break laws, while others are ostracized, sued, and even arrested for breaking no law except political correctness—and the media does not object.

They explain why groups like Antifa and BLM are able to function outside the law, terrorizing communities and cities with impunity—and few in the black communities object.

These principles explain why those with different cultural viewpoints are held to different legal standards depending on whether those viewpoints come from the Right or the Left—and few in the legal profession object.

These principles explain why new forms of intolerance, fanaticism, cruelty, illegality, and discrimination are becoming widespread against those of a conservative worldview, why these practices are protected and praised—and secularists do not object.

These principles explain why reverse-racism is not condemned but is encouraged as beneficial for society—and no one objects.

These principles explain why modern strategies of prejudicial treatment of conservatives and Christians are not merely allowed but supported and aided by academia, the media, and government—and few in any liberal community object.

These principles explain why the killing of unborns is justified—and legions of progressives cheer.

These principles explain why logically impossible ideas like gender choice are normalized—and parents and educators applaud the advances of self-determinism and do not object.

These principles explain why mutilation of the human body to reverse immutable biological anatomy is hailed as heroic—and the medical community does not object.

These principles explain why traditional Christian standards of right and wrong are excoriated as bigoted and hateful, while woke standards of hatefulness, injustice, prejudice, and favoritism are acclaimed as enlightened—and the champions of justice do not object.

These principles explain why freedom of choice is one-sided—and so few object to the double standard.

These principles explain why businesses and educational institutions, secure in the sanction of the Emperor of Progressivism,* are allowed and encouraged to discriminate as long as they do so against the right constituencies—and the justice department does not object.

These principles explain why the judgmentalism, narrow-mindedness, hate speech, bias, and religiophobia of the emperor's legions are considered virtuous as long as they are directed against conservatives—and liberals do not object.

These principles explain why those who suggest that the emperor advocating these violations against virtue is not merely an emperor without clothes but an evil phantom. They are lambasted, ostracized, silenced, and, if possible, destroyed—and no one objects.

The principles of these chapters explain why history may judge this generation of Americans to have been a population of lemmings that lost the capacity to think judiciously, logically, and implicationally, a generation that trampled absolutes underfoot, a generation that

---

* For those who may not recognize it, the reference is to Hans Christian Andersen's *The Emperor's New Clothes.*

lost its moral and ethical compass and allowed history's greatest nation to flounder into oblivion.

They explain why this nation is at a cultural and moral crossroads and is rapidly approaching a point of no return.

6

PREPAREDNESS
the unvirtue: indifference

My concern is not whether God is on our side;
my greatest concern is to be on God's side, for God is always right.
— Abraham Lincoln

The United States is on the brink of an ideological civil war.
In 2007, then Pope Benedict XVI said the crisis of the West was a crisis of truth.[1] Concerned Americans needed to wake up to the reality of this deepening crisis before the war consumes them. Otherwise they would never know what hit them.

Whether or not another major armed conflict—a world war or something like it—will draw American civilians into it personally to the same extent as did the wars of the past century, no one can foresee. Possibly that will occur. If it does, however, it will surely look much different than previous wars. It may be a long-distance war, a technological war, a chemical or biowar, or even—God forbid, though no one knows what will happen when terrorists lay their hands on the bomb—a nuclear war.

Prevention and Preparation

We cannot predict any of that. Experts, scientists, military leaders, diplomats, and politicians are constantly both *preparing* for such contingencies and doing everything they can in their specific fields to *prevent* them.

But the average man in the street cannot prevent them. The forces that lead to war are outside our control. Nor can we do much to *prepare* for them other than, as the saying goes, making sure our own houses are in order.

Personally in order—families, relationships, marriages, finances, and our relationship with our Maker. Beyond this, we simply have to live our lives faithfully, with integrity, keeping relationships sound, doing to and for others as we would be done by, and—though it sounds fatalistic—hope and pray for the best.

We cannot prevent the coming ideological war either. It is definitely on the way. The ominous signs of its approach loom on the horizon.

Though the coming war will be a different kind of war, it's one we *can* and *must* prepare for. If we're prudent, watchful, and willing, we can protect and shield ourselves from its most brutal and vicious fallout. What will be its ultimate impact upon the future of America remains for history to determine.

Actually this war has already begun. We are still in the early phases. Sides, forces, unwritten pacts, political and societal factions, and back-room diplomacies are still in flux. But as these complex groupings, partnerships, bonds, and alliances come into focus and sort themselves out, sooner or later we will all be drawn into the conflict.

The parallel to the years leading up to World War II is more fitting than it may seem. During the 1930s, considerable minority support for the Nazi cause existed in Great Britain, even within the royal family. It took time for sides and loyalties to clarify themselves. By 1940, except for a few spies and Nazi sympathizers, the war had two sides that were well defined.

We are in a similar pre-outbreak phase of the approaching ideological war mentioned earlier. Causes and agendas continue to shift. Many of the ideologies involved and the alliances that will ultimately form between distinct but occasionally overlapping agendas remain fluid. Much remains in the incubational stage.

But the ideologies, alliances, programs, long-range goals, and priorities and methods are steadily solidifying and coming into focus.

The sides, cleavages, and tactics grow sharper and more defined every year. War has been declared, and hostilities will continue to get worse and worse.

Weapons of Warfare

An actual "war" in the sense in which we usually use the word is relatively straightforward. All wars are horrific, but they are usually reasonably clear-cut: country vs. country, army vs. army, kill or be killed, mano a mano. One side wins; the other eventually lays down its arms. This is obviously simplistic. Wars like Vietnam and the Hundred Years War in Europe are more complicated, sometimes without clear resolution. But in a war where national conquest and defeating the opposite side with weapons of warfare is the objective (even if not the *sole* objective), we can *do* specific things to prepare for them. Preparation, in a sense, may be very practical.

If an army is advancing on your country, those threatened take up weapons to protect themselves and fight back. Even as I write these words in 2022, this reality is being played out for the whole world to see in Ukraine. Obviously the weapons of warfare have varied through the years, from bows and arrows and boiling oil poured from the top of castles to guns and artillery and cannons and tanks and navies to sophisticated stealth bombers, self-guided missiles, and now drones. But the idea is the same—meet force with force. It's kill or be killed.

With modernity has come a whole new range of terrible weapons. But certain preparatory steps are still possible.

If a chemical attack is imminent, gas masks and safe zones become very practical measures.

If biological weapons are used—which the COVID-19 pandemic taught us—another whole range of protocols are put in place to meet the threat and protect the populace.

If the attack comes on computer systems, firewalls and backup measures—and backups to the backups—become the first line of defense.

If a nuclear war is predicted, bomb shelters may be the preparation some will choose. Many underground bunkers were indeed constructed in the U.S. during the 1950s and 1960s. I remember them. The fear was real, and people built real underground bunkers out of steel and foot-thick concrete.

The coming ideological war, however, will be completely different. No such easily identifiable and straightforward measures of preparation will accomplish much. The weapons of the coming war will be harder to see, subtle, disguised, often invisible. They will not be weapons designed to *kill* but cunningly devised and employed to make their opponents *think* in certain ways.

The battle will be to control *minds and hearts,* not territories or economies or resources.

The indifferent and unprepared victims in this new war will never be aware they are being targeted, never recognize the stealth weapons being used against them. Thus they never realize, even as the war is being carried out, that they are being silently conquered by an invisible enemy.

Those thought-weapons are already in widespread use all around us. They infiltrate our homes through our televisions for hours every day. The battle has been going on for years. In our nation's universities, the war is already over. As it spreads into the general culture, every year the thought-weapons that have been so successful from colleges to kindergartens are being used against us and against those we love, against our churches, against our freedoms, against our children, and are becoming more subtle, more devious, more cunning—and more effective.

But few are paying attention.

Ideas Not Guns

Though they may be taken over by them, no one was ever *killed* by an idea. True, it is ideas that lead to armed warfare. However, ideas themselves kill no one. Ideas have consequences and lead to actions.

Look at how many deaths the *idea* that unborn babies are not fully human has led to. Evil ideas have evil consequences.

Whether the ideas of the coming ideological war will lead to open conflict in a traditional sense, we cannot know. But nonetheless, it will be a war that determines the course of our nation's future.

It will be a war of ideas not guns. An internal war. A war that pits Americans against Americans.

A new *civil war.*

Right-thinking men and women *must* prepare for it by recognizing the adversary. It is imperative that *Americans* who value the principles that have been the strength of our nation, along with dedicated *Christians,* prepare for it together. The alliance between these two constituencies represents the only bulwark able to withstand America's new internal adversary.

Progressivism's Agenda:
A Replacement Secularized Nation

The objective of that adversary is to do away with the nation of the United States as it was established and put in its place a replacement nation founded on completely secular principles. They may still choose to call it the "United States of America." But it will be a new nation built on a new and different foundation bearing almost no resemblance to the nation founded in 1776 and 1789.

Two groups—traditional Americans and dedicated Christians— are all that can stop the formation of the replacement nation. They will be at the very forefront of the battle. If Christians especially do not take measures to prepare, and soon, they will witness massive casualties throughout Christendom. Marriages and families and Christian congregations will be torn apart. The relational devastation and catastrophic ruin brought to churches will be widespread. Much of it may be beyond healing.

It has been customary to use the term *post-Christian* to describe America in the third millennium. In a sense this is true. But while secularism has seemingly triumphed over Christianity in the culture and society at large, the cause of Christ is far from dead.

True Christianity—Gone

Characterizing the new war will be the attempt of modern humanistic secularism in America to irrevocably eradicate our historic Christian ideals, to deal the final death blow to Christian influence in America.

One of the most glaring examples is the Trojan horse of the LGBTQ agenda, currently infiltrating Christianity from within—normalizing everything that agenda wants within Christian churches, redefining its clergy, its regulations, its marriage practices, and its entire outlook on the human condition. The LGBTQ agenda is already well on its way to eviscerating the Christianity of the New Testament.

A ruthless and sinister enemy has invaded the church of Jesus Christ, yet most Christians continue going to church Sunday after Sunday with no idea they themselves are in the crosshairs of a cultural battle to do away with *Gospel-Commands-Obedience-Christianity* altogether.

American Values and Christendom

The ideological war, however, is not purely a "religious" conflict. Because the influence of generally Christian values have suffused the principles that make America what it is, even so-called secular American men and women who lament the loss of that traditional root-value system will find themselves allied with Christians in the battle. The worldview and outlook on life and culture will be shared by Christians and traditional-thinking American men and women who may not consider themselves especially religious. Dedicated Christians and generally conservative traditional Americans share a similar undergirding outlook on life, culture, and what America as a nation of light and exceptionalism in the world has been and ought to continue to be. Thus they will find themselves on the same side in the ideological war.

This highlights the complexity of the alliances presently shifting and changing. A conservative and traditional-thinking non-Christian may be fighting alongside fundamentalist evangelicals and conservative Protestants and Catholics, while a liberal gay who acknowledges Christian beliefs finds himself fighting alongside progressive secularists. The battle lines will be murky and obscure.

Forces have been lining up on the two sides for generations. While the Nazi takeover of Germany and buildup to World War II took two decades (roughly 1920–40), the coming ideological war has been in the invisible buildup phase for almost half a century.

The climax is now approaching. It will be fought over the ideas, virtues, and the traditional values of the Christian faith, which in large measure represent the founding root system and ongoing fabric and strength of the United States as a nation.

7

ALERTNESS
the unvirtue: lethargy

Propaganda helps change the world by creating a false impression
of the way the world is . . . . [T]he mainstream media is framing the general
public's understanding of news and events according to what was until
very recently a radical ideology confined to left-wing intellectual elites.
— Rod Dreher

Few people, no matter how just the cause, relish the idea of taking up arms and actually *killing* another human being. There may be a few such individuals, but they are relatively rare. Certainly wives, mothers, and sisters are even less eager to see their husbands, sons, and brothers take up arms, not thinking of the enemy as much as they are the terror of losing their *own* boys and men. And now in recent years, women taking up arms are included in that fear.

Ideas As Weapons

In a very real way, however, it may be easier to take up a gun than to engage in the world of ideas. The enemy in an armed conflict is easy to see, identifiable. It's him or me, so to speak, on the field of battle. Horrifying as is the thought of killing or being killed, that battle instinct is more straightforward. Most men are able to face it with courage. Something within a man's innate psyche is able to rise to the primal challenge to defend one's life, family, home, and country. It's something many women have never understood—that they have hated about the men they love—the time that comes when a man says, "Sometimes a man's gotta do what a man's gotta do."*

Millions of young men from all over the world eagerly signed up and were sent off to the battles of World War II, full of gusto and bravado to take on the enemy. By the time Normandy came, that bravado had waned. But thousands of soldiers still did their duty. Doing one's duty, even with death staring him in the face, is another thing that "a man's gotta do."

The coming war will be fought over ideas. *That* will be the battleground, not national borders or world power or territorial domination or control of natural resources. Its primary weapons will not be guns, tanks, chemicals, toxins, airplanes, armies, drones, viruses, navies, missiles, or bombs. More subtle tactics will be used to sway opinion and win the war of ideas.

Argument and persuasion, of course, are always the weapons of choice in a war of ideas, but they are singularly ineffective. Few people are persuaded by direct frontal assault. Opposing sides become more entrenched by argument, not convinced. Both sides fight for their convictions in the idea-battle with logic and reasoning that to them are utterly convincing. But their opponents only dig in deeper and hurl back their own opposing arguments. It's the equivalent of the ten-month-long Battle of Verdun in World War I. Though there are always casualties (750,000 at Verdun), few clear-cut winners emerge from trench warfare in any battle of ideas.

The heavy artillery in a battle of ideas is often invisible. One may think *truth* is the major weapon in the idea war, but it is not so. Though both sides claim—and believe to the bottom of their hearts—that their ideas represent truth, and they are arguing for and standing up for truth; in fact, truth is often one of the first casualties of battle. If truth later emerges as a by-product of the conflict, it is in such shambles it is hardly recognizable as what is called "truth." Though the evil of Nazism was ultimately defeated—which might be considered

---

* *Duty* and its antonym might be considered another endangered virtue in our time. Many such virtues are endangered, but unfortunately space does not allow us to consider them in more detail.

a victory of right over wrong—the war cost some fifty million human lives and left Stalin and a ruthless communist elite in power, arguably no less evil than Nazism. To what extent is "truth" represented by that outcome? No doubt the war had to be fought to stop Nazism. But that is a philosophical question in which "truth" becomes very ambiguous.

To repeat, counterintuitive as it seems, truth also becomes a casualty in the idea war. Many of the tactics and weapons used in the idea war are not based in truth at all. Indeed, they often *obscure* truth. The objective in the idea war, as in an armed conflict, is not truth at all but *victory*—my idea vanquishing your idea.

It is idea vs. idea. Early in the ideological tussle, both sides to some extent stop asking what is true and ask only how they can win the argument. Truth becomes trampled underfoot in the quest for victory.*

Propaganda—Right, Wrong, and Truth in War

One of two opposing ideas may indeed be *closer* to the truth. Five is closer to the truth of two plus two than sixteen. But it still cannot be called *truth*. In the wars of history, it may be that truth is more represented on one side or the other. It is often said in a war that everyone believes God is on their side. But most Americans and Christians would say truth was more represented in the Second World War on the side of the Allies. It is difficult to believe that a sound, logical, humane case can be made for the veracity of the Nazi cause and the murder of six million Jews. That is obviously a somewhat subjective perspective. Even if it is true, however, fifty million deaths was a terrible price to pay.

---

* Both rhetoric and dialectic are used in the war of ideas. Dialectic involves discussion between those holding different points of view who are attempting objectively to arrive at truth through reasoned argumentation and debate rather than emotional and persuasive tactics. Rhetoric, on the other hand, uses speech and writing techniques, including exaggeration, for the express purposes of persuading listeners to a particular point of view. Truth, therefore, is not necessarily a fundamental requirement for the effective use of rhetoric.

For a war's aggressor, *propaganda* is a weapon of choice. Both sides may accuse the other of propaganda. But again, some ideas are closer to truth than others. Propaganda is generally defined as using misleading, exaggerated, or outright false information (extreme forms of rhetoric) to bolster and enforce a political cause or point of view. Accusing the *other* side of propaganda becomes a key propaganda point.

But though both sides vehemently believe their own propaganda, an objective historical perspective usually reveals the difference. The Nazi propaganda, "Jews are evil," is obviously different than the Allied slogan, "Careless talk costs lives." Wikipedia defines the latter as a wartime "propaganda campaign" by the British government. But that is not the case. The two so-called propagandas were not created equal. During the Second World War, careless talk *did* cost lives. The statement was a *true* statement, while that of the Nazis was patently false. In Wikipedia's definition can be clearly detected the not-so-subtle revisionism that is one of the key ingredients of modernism's idea-war strategy—denigrating the history of the West.

Progressivism is fond of accusing conservatives of "misinformation." The charge is one of progressivism's most potent and lethal accusations. That tactic itself, however, is misinformation. Progressivism's misinformation is far more destructive than that of conservatives. But since the Left is far more adept at passing off its misinformation as fact, its lies slide into the culture invisibly. All the while, the media beats the drum of the often imaginary misinformation coming from conservatives. As said earlier, the ideological war is already underway around us in a thousand ways. The Wikipedia statement about Britain's WWII "propaganda" is but a tiny example.

In any war of ideas, what both sides call propaganda flies furiously in every direction. It takes mental (and spiritual) alertness to discern who is misleading whom. Often the aggressor is the party most guilty of (often false) propaganda ("Jews are evil"; "The Sudetenland rightfully belongs to us") in order to justify their aggression.

Yet *all* of an aggressor's points may not be entirely false. Many in Britain and the U.S. indeed felt that Germany had been dealt a raw deal at Versailles after World War I and some of its territorial claims were justified. Hitler, of course, used those territorial claims to launch an attempted takeover of the whole of Europe. He manipulated the territorial argument (partially true, perhaps, at root) into an *untrue* propaganda weapon to justify the invasion of Germany's neighbors. This highlights the point that even misleading propaganda, when used by an aggressor to launch a war, is not always 100 percent black and white.

When used as weapons, though some ideas are more true than others, by their very nature ideas are slippery commodities, subject to almost infinite variety of interpretation and nuance. Hence, Wikipedia's using the term *propaganda* to describe a vitally *true* and necessary-information campaign.

Such will increasingly be the tactics against Christians and traditional-values Americans as the idea war accelerates. In today's culture much true and necessary information being pointed out by knowledgeable and intelligent conservatives about many issues is labeled as *mis*information and their voices silenced. About abortion, transathletics, global warming, gender-change operations, and COVID vaccines, what progressives hate more than anything is scientific truth that does not confirm their agenda. So they label science that counters their politically correct interpretations misinformation.

8

DISCERNING THE SIGNS OF THE TIMES
the unvirtue: unmindfulness

Those who do not learn from history are doomed to repeat it.
— George Santayana

The above familiar quote by Spanish-American philosopher, essayist, and novelist Jorge Agustín Nicolás Ruiz de Santayana y Borrás, known in English as George Santayana (1863–1952), probably originally read, "Those who cannot remember the past are condemned to repeat it." We might fruitfully also remind ourselves of Jesus's words in Matthew 16:3b: "You know how to interpret the appearance of the sky, but you cannot interpret the signs of the times."

This chapter, in a sense, represents part 2 of "Alertness," emphasizing the importance of wakefulness and watchfulness, pinching ourselves to make sure we don't mentally go to sleep. If we're not mindful of what is taking place around us, as a people we will lazily drift into a whole series of unvirtues. Then it's game over. History will repeat. Germany in the 1930s—an entire nation asleep at the wheel because its people did not discern the signs of the times.

There is a vital historical component to alertness and wakefulness. Understanding virtue requires being a student of history. People, nations, cultures, movements, religions, even ideas, progress through ebbs and flows through the decades, through the centuries. Virtue, too, ebbs and flows. Nations, even whole civilizations, rise and fall on the basis of their mindfulness of the past, their attentiveness to virtue, and their perception of what is taking place around them and their response to their times.

The U.S. Civil War and World War II are vital to our understanding of how virtue works and what happens when it fades. Virtue *requires* reading the signs of the times and discerning what is occurring in our cultural world at our own particular time in history.

The Murky American Tragedy

Most wars are not as clear cut as World War II. The American Civil War typifies the usual case. More than a century and a half later the debate continues over which side was right and which was wrong. Propaganda (and information and *mis*information) continues to fly. In one sense (though *only* one), it was a very religious war. Both sides felt they were fighting for righteousness and truth—620,000 deaths and 150 years of analyses have still not settled that debate. There is no universal consensus in the opposing series of ideas that was "closer to the truth." Even the matter of which side was the "aggressor" remains hotly debated. Though the fact is always a serious consideration in any war, it is far from as simple as who fired the first shot.

The subject of the U.S. Civil War is more complex than the Second World War because the ideas are more complex. Those ideas are so thoroughly interwoven that they are impossible to untangle in a straightforward, black-and-white way. It was not simply North vs. South. There was also a less strident East vs. West component, centered around the question whether new states admitted to the Union would be slave or free. This highlighted the political component, as relevant today as it was then—the balance of power in the Senate.

Of course slavery itself lay at the root of many of the arguments too—whether slavery was right or wrong. Christians were divided on the issue. The racial divide—black and white—obviously factored into this question. And powerful business interests (the role of "king cotton" in the flourishing economy of the South) viewed slavery in business, not human, terms.

And of course the constitutional issue of states' rights plunged straight to the heart of the origins of the U.S. democracy and republic.

It was *very* complicated. Feelings (and the propaganda) were intense from all these directions, which explains the ferocity of the war. It surely represents America's great national tragedy.

Discerning the signs of the times, it does not take great insight to recognize that the ideological war upon us today is also a "civil war" and already bears many of the same hallmarks of America's 1860s Civil War. It may be that civil wars are more fierce than inter-nation wars because the ideas and personalities are so close to home. Nothing quite compares with the rancor within families or the hatred of the divorced wife toward her ex-husband. Though it should break our hearts, families can fight more bitterly than any social groups on the planet.

In family battles, too, truth is more often a casualty than a relational compass in the attempt to find amiable solutions that preserve healthy relationships. Sadly, it is inevitable that such rancor and bitterness will also characterize the accelerating ideological war. The current political acrimony between Republicans and Democrats represents but the opening sorties in a war that will become far more malicious, vindictive, and hostile even than the venom hurled at Donald Trump and his supporters during the past three-quarters of a decade.

The Tactical Weapons of Idea-Warfare

As was true of America's former Civil War, truth is just as difficult to discern today. Legitimate science labeled as misinformation by both the Left and the Right shows that we are already there.

Truth is a casualty because the tactics and weapons of idea-warfare often involve the very opposite of truth. The fact that the goal is not to discover truth but victory—to *vanquish* opposing ideas—requires the use of weapons, by their very nature, that cast truth aside. Propaganda and control of the media is usually the first of these. To its aid are brought the weapons of condescension, ridicule, brainwashing, deception, exaggeration, distortion of facts, lying, and manipulation of evidence, all of which may lead to threats, coercion, isolation, removal of freedoms, and imprisonment.

These many weapons are used—perhaps more maliciously, though not exclusively, by the aggressor—not to find truth but to crush and ultimately kill opposing ideas. They are *seriously* effective weapons.

Germany in the 1920s and 1930s demonstrated just how successful these tactics can be in the minds of an *undiscerning* people who were *not* reading the signs of the times. By the late 1930s, most of Germany idolized Hitler. Six million Jews died as testimony to the success of Hitler's tactical weaponry of propaganda and brainwashing to normalize hideous and horrifying ideas within the hearts and brains of Germany's military and civilian population.

The ideological war will be no less intent on killing than were the combatants in World War II. The objective will be to *kill* and eradicate the ideas of Christianity and traditional historic American standards. They must be killed to establish the Secular Replacement Nation. To accomplish that end, these same tactics will be used. It will not matter who is hurt, who is ostracized, who is lied about, whose freedoms are taken away, whose reputations are destroyed, whose lives are ruined.

Misinformation

Though eradicating the past's ideas and standards will not be everyone's objective, this will be the single-minded goal of the most militant in the ideological war.

Yet an imperative point must not be forgotten: otherwise good and honorable people will be engaged on *both* sides, convinced they are standing for truth. Many, however, mentally lethargic and not alert to truth, will be deceived by a subtle and devious propaganda campaign of untrue misinformation.

How many gullible Americans and Christians watching network news night after night have been slowly brainwashed into thinking that Republicans, conservatives, and evangelical Christians are guilty *en masse* of misinformation when in fact the very opposite is the case. Most of the misinformation spreading through the culture has originated from the Left. It is another of progressivism's dirty little secrets. The propaganda war is underway, and millions are believing the untruths of misinformation coming from progressivism.

People gullibly absorb and accept misinformation because they are not students of history. They are not discerning the signs of the times. They do not see that the Left is using the same tactics to manipulate the media to its agenda used in the 1930s to put the nation of Germany to sleep.

Is it judgmental to say that the propaganda of misinformation is more deceitfully used by the Left than the Right? Any intelligent individual can see that it is so. Gender misinformation is but one example. There are *not* seventy-two genders. It is blatantly and scientifically *untrue*. The multigender illusion is but one of many lies of misinformation being spread through the media as true. Conservative thinkers, still weighing evidence factually, continue to say that (except for *extreme* abnormalities) there are *two* biological birth sexual orientations.

Who is guilty of spreading misinformation?

I Will Be Progressivism's Enemy; No Human Being Is *My* Enemy

To many on the front lines leading the charge from the Left—especially the LGBTQ community, which stands at the vanguard of the progressive offensive—conservative Christians and traditional-values Americans are nothing less than *enemies*. Those who are not alive to the virtue of cultural alertness will either be bulldozed into submission and compliance with progressivism's agenda, though they know it is wrong, or will unthinkingly be swept into its ranks as foot soldiers against friends, relatives, and fellow church members. They may never know they have silently been conscripted into an army whose goal is the destruction of the Christian faith and the historic underpinnings of their country.

Having thus spoken boldly, let me return to this reminder: no man or woman of that army is my enemy. Many will consider *me* an enemy, but they are not mine. Some of the *ideas* of the agenda of misinformation and untruth I may consider evil enough to call those ideas *enemies* of the truth. But the men and women deceived by those ideas are not. Many of them (thankfully not all) may also treat you as an enemy for the ideas *you* hold. Nevertheless, it is possible for you to affirm the same truth—they are not your enemies.

Progressivism as an idea, as an agenda for cultural change, is ruthless. It will do *anything* to vanquish those who oppose it. Make no mistake—that is what Christians and traditional Americans are in for. We will be the *enemies* of the most stalwart and malicious of progressives.

But *truth* is never ruthless. Truth is unyielding but never ruthless. No man or woman is *our* enemy. They are brothers and sisters of our common humanity who need to be loved into recognition of the deceptions that hold them captive.

9

FOUNDATIONS
the unvirtue: chance

*They above others improve most in all virtue, who endeavor
to overcome those things which are most grievous and contrary unto them.
Be careful to avoid with great diligence those things in yourself
which do commonly displease you in others.*

— Thomas à Kempis

How, then, do we exercise the virtues of *preparedness*, *alertness*, and *discernment* to make ourselves ready for what is coming. How do we "alertly prepare" for ideological war.

By laying wise idea-foundations rooted in implicational thinking.

Foundations are the bedrock of everything. Whatever you undertake must have a foundation well laid if you want the result to look like what you envisioned—build a house, make a bookshelf, write a book, paint a picture, remodel a kitchen, plant a garden, play the piano, take a trip, start a business, hang a picture on the wall, build a new nation . . . everything.

Understanding *ideas* requires a foundation too. Building a life on virtue requires the most important foundation of all: a foundation of character. Building a country and sustaining its strength requires a foundation too—one of *national* virtue and character. But as America approaches the second quarter of the third millennium, that national foundation is crumbling.

The Random Flow of Opinion

We're assaulted by ideas all day long. Most of us take them as they come. Our thought-foundations are built hit-or-miss by chance. They are thus weak foundations—flimsy, unsound, arbitrary, and incomplete. Then we form judgments and opinions from that random flow of ideas. We rarely stop to give thought to whether they're good or bad ideas, or even *true* ideas. We simply absorb them. Chance dictates most of the ideas we encounter, and thus chance is also a prime mover in determining the conclusions we draw.

Our range of opinions has been formed by thousands of ideas blowing through our brains haphazardly, year after year. Out of this vast pool of idea-input, we gradually assume that those ideas we have adopted as our own, our opinions, are true.

However, we don't usually think much about the mental and intellectual skills necessary to produce *wise* thinking and *sound* judgment, or the ability to discern good ideas from bad ideas. What if my selection process in evaluating that pool of ideas flooding my brain is faulty?

That raises a huge question few people ask of themselves: Which of my own opinions *aren't* true?

Implications

Implicational thinking seldom enters into this process. What are the *implications* of the ideas I have been exposed to when followed to their logical endpoint? Implicational thinking is not taught in school. It's not taught in church. It's not listed among the qualifications for the presidency (though maybe it should be!).

The skill to think judiciously, wisely, objectively, and implicationally about ideas simply isn't one of the highly valued virtues of our society. In more than seventeen years of schooling, I do not once recall hearing a single mention made of developing the skill to *think* objectively and implicationally. The sole emphasis from kindergarten to graduate school was to absorb the ideas and opinions being taught, not learn to *think* wisely. That's why my wife and I homeschooled our sons, and why the number of Christian schools and classical schools and homeschools has mushroomed—because of the dearth of *true* education in the progressive school system. This has also been my experience in church. Take what others teach about doctrine and theology, accept their opinions as true because they say so. But do not *think* for yourself. I have been battling most of my adult life against the taboo of thinking implicationally about the ideas of Christianity.

This same process, with accompanying taboos, exists in the world of political ideas. We know this fact all too well. We're expected to go along with the accepted ideas our particular group teaches. Do *not* think outside the box.

That is the greatest taboo of all. Ask anyone in the news business or educational systems who happens to voice a conservative idea. Groups don't like their people straying from the approved orthodoxy.

Truth

Implications always follow foundations. If mental, intellectual, and spiritual foundations are well laid, with an approach to ideas based on something more trustworthy than personal opinion—including opinions we're told we're *supposed* to believe—then objective thinking will usually lead in the direction of truth.

But that's not easy. We all function from day to day in various groupthink boxes. Progressing far along the road toward truth may take breaking out of those boxes. That's why it is so difficult to build sound thought-foundations. We have to seek foundations more solidly rooted than the opinions in our groupthink boxes.

If you have read this far, it will be obvious that by the word *truth* I do not mean opinions masquerading as what someone might *call* truth. Opinions do not equal truth. The two *may* coincide, or they may not. That I *think* something is true (my opinion) does not make it true. Many of the majority opinions in our individual groupthink boxes may be true. But just as many probably aren't.

In the exchange of ideas in today's highly charged climate, the ability to lay aside personal opinion in favor of the higher objective of engaging serious thought in trying to discern *real truth*—which may not coincide at every point with the range of approved opinions in the boxes—is a rarely demonstrated characteristic of personal maturity.

Why do I call foundations themselves a "virtue"?

Because the practice and skill of building wise foundations in life is a virtuous character quality. We need look no further than the biblical book of Proverbs. We might go so far as to call it the *foundational* virtue upon which other virtues grow and deepen.

Nowhere is the virtue of building wise foundations more important than in learning how to think about *ideas* with acuity—rationally, objectively, and implicationally.

We come back to *ideas*. Understanding ideas requires foundations.

Why do I think the way I do? Upon what do I base the conclusions I form? Are my foundations solid? Are my *opinions* well founded?

A Multitude of Voices

Many voices have been articulating similar warnings as those in this book for years. I am but one humbly following in their footsteps, choosing to focus my own perspective through the lens of virtue. Two of the recent titles I am most familiar with are from Rod Dreher, author of the 2017 bestseller *The Benedict Option*. In 2020, Dreher published a sequel whose title was taken from Aleksandr Solzhenitsyn's challenge to the Russian people on the day of his arrest in 1974.

Dreher used Solzhenitsyn's exact words, titling his new work *Live Not by Lies*. In both his books, in broad strokes, Dreher takes up Solzhenitsyn's banner, challenging serious Christians:

- to awaken to the disintegration of America's historic spiritual underpinnings;
- to recognize the attacks on religious liberty inundating Christians wherever they turn;

- to courageously determine not to placidly accept the false ideas being normalized by the cultural trends of progressivism, and;
- to discover personal and communal ways to draw apart from the world's systems, politics, perspectives, and lifestyles in order to keep themselves, their families, their churches, and their Christian communities energetically alive and based on scriptural truth.*

As the title suggests, sixth-century St. Benedict of Nursia served as the model for Dreher's earlier book. In the face of the depravity and decadence of the collapsing Roman Empire, Benedict and the monks who followed him during the coming centuries built monasteries that grew into vibrant, stable, hospitable communities for Christians. In the words of the book's cover, these centers for learning and community "were strongholds of light through the Dark Ages." Dreher adds, "they saved not just Christianity but also Western Civilization."

Our challenge is to find practical ways to follow Benedict's example—not by monastic escapism but through means suitable to the times, but nonetheless effective against the threats of our *own* era. If we can find those practicalities, it may not be too late also to save biblical Christianity in our time, as a spiritual and cultural "dark age" sweeps over us.

Dreher does not only reference *Saint* Benedict; he likewise views former *Pope* Benedict as a worthy prophetic successor to his namesake's mantle.

He writes:

> Pope Emeritus Benedict XVI foretells a world in which the church will live in small circles of committed believers who live the faith intensely, and who will have to be somewhat cut off from mainstream society for the sake of holding on to the truth. . . . [I]n 2012, the then-pontiff

---

* These four represent *my* broad interpretation of his overarching message. The details are clearly far more complex and far reaching than these. (Rod Dreher, *Live Not by Lies* [New York: Sentinel Books, Random House, 2020].)

said that the spiritual crisis overtaking the West is the most serious since the fall of the Roman Empire near the end of the fifth century. The light of Christianity is flickering out all over the West. There are people alive today who may live to see the effective death of Christianity within our civilization.[1]

Pope Benedict's place in the discussion is so significant that he deserves an entire chapter devoted to his role. That will be reserved for later.

In *Live Not by Lies*, taking Solzhenitsyn for his inspiration, Dreher's challenge concerns the cancerous falsehoods of the current "spiritual dark age" mentioned above that is closing in upon thinking Christians who take the *ideas* and *implications* of their faith with life-regulating seriousness.

The coming dark age may not be brought about by a collapsing empire as in St. Benedict's day or by a ruthless dictatorial regime such as that of the Soviet Union, which imprisoned Solzhenitsyn. It is a dark age built on *ideas*. A dark age the former pope calls a spiritual crisis unlike any seen for fifteen hundred years.

A crisis characterized by:

- false ideas masquerading as truth;
- dark ideas masquerading as light;
- unscriptural and illogical ideas;
- foolish ideas;
- depraved ideas;
- hedonistic ideas masquerading as rational, intelligent, fashionable, liberating, and enlightened thinking; and/or
- ideas that, once the masks are torn off, are nothing more nor less than *lies*.

These are all bound up in a package of lies that modernity insists everyone embrace, accept in others—and call truth.

Dreher writes:

What did it mean to live by lies? It meant, Solzhenitsyn writes, accepting without protest all the falsehoods and propaganda that the state compelled its citizens to affirm . . . to get along peaceably under totalitarianism. Everybody says that they have no choice but to conform, says Solzhenitsyn, and to accept powerlessness. But that is the lie that gives all the other lies their malign force. The ordinary man may not be able to overturn the kingdom of lies, but he can at least say that he is not going to be its loyal subject.[2]

I may not say much here that can be added to the succinct gauntlet Solzhenitsyn laid down. He and many of those who have taken up his banner have articulated it with power and precision.*

A Spiritual Orientation

At the same time, however, I recognize that I view our present culture through some different lenses than others. Most of the authors mentioned in the footnote below are involved in the political arena and write about politics. I have never written about politics in my life. I do not view the world primarily through that lens. I have been paying close attention to the political world for fifty years, but politics is not my reference point.

---

* This is an appropriate opportunity to emphasize exactly this point, that the message of this book is not particularly unique or original. As noted, a multitude of voices since Francis Schaeffer's time have strenuously decried the loss of absolutes, and many others are likewise articulating cultural warnings to Americans and Christians. I would especially note *The Book of Absolutes* by William Gairdner, *The Death of Truth* by Dennis McCallum, *A Refutation of Moral Relativism* by Peter Kreeft, *The Gnostic Empire Strikes Back* by Peter Jones, *The Fall of Christendom and the Separation of the Remnant* by Frank McEleny, *Whatever Happened to Truth?* by Andreas Köstenberger et al., *Beheading Hydra: A Radical Plan for Christians in an Atheistic Age* by Fr. Dwight Longenecker, and *Assailing the Gates of Hell: Christianity at War with the Left* by Jan Adriaan Schlebusch. This volume happens to be my personal "testimonial," so to speak, reinforcing what many other voices have been saying for years.

The fundamental orientation I bring to my personal life and writing is a spiritual and scriptural orientation. A spiritual worldview thoroughly informs these works I have mentioned, a perspective which, in the specific case of Solzhenitsyn and Dreher, is communicated through the prism of their Orthodox system of belief. Though the label is inaccurate in many respects, I have come from an *evangelical* background. These distinctions create inevitable nuances that influence how all of us who are sounding these warnings interpret truth and culture and the conclusions we draw. It may be that my different frame of reference will prove a useful addition to the discussion about how Christians should respond to the deluge of secularization engulfing them.

I realize of course that *all* labels are held in suspicion by those occupying different places on the spectrum. The "evangelical" label has had it pretty rough in recent years. The political Left often characterizes evangelicals as unthinking, bigoted, racist, backward Neanderthals. Similar judgments are leveled against *anyone* holding conservative perspectives. But conservative evangelicals seem to represent a more appealing target than secular conservatives.

So perhaps the *E* word will cause some to close this book. But it is good to get it out in the open, so you know who I am and what is my background. This said, however, in all honesty I have not discovered such clear articulation of the imperative for Christians to separate themselves from the downward moral slide of the world in evangelicalism as I have from these two Orthodox men and the former Catholic pope, to whose legacy, as I said, we will later devote an entire chapter.

As to the *C* word, I do *not* characterize myself as a political "conservative." My perspectives on a range of issues, as well as my voting record, would probably surprise most readers. Much of what has already been said may sound conservative to some. But there are those who also consider me far too *liberal* for their tastes. I have no political agenda—liberal *or* conservative. I think through every issue and position on its own merits, building my foundations on truth, and working my way up from there. My views—spiritual, cultural, political—fit no convenient mold.

My only agenda is to find truth—*real* truth, even where it may not coincide exactly with my opinions, or yours, on every issue or interpretation. Those conclusions may occasionally fall on that liberal–conservative spectrum in unexpected places. I don't live very comfortably in groupthink boxes.

10

CIVILITY
the unvirtue: anger

When the norm is decency, other virtues can thrive:
integrity, honesty, compassion, kindness, and trust.
— Raja Krishnamoorthi

One of the glaring and unfortunate results of the cultural and political divide in which our nation finds itself is a divisive spirit of hostility between those of differing perspective. Anger toward those with whom we disagree, while not new, has taken over as the new normal. The entire relational chemistry is toxic. We justify such hostility because each of us is convinced with every gray cell in our brains that our idea-adversaries (many would go so far as to call them *enemies*) are so blatantly and stubbornly *wrong*. The clash of ideas on both sides thus takes on the harsh timbre of a holy war—of *righteous* anger, *justified* anger, *necessary* anger.

There is, of course, such a thing as righteous anger—Jesus overturned the tables of the moneychangers. But the argumentative and antagonistic spirit poisoning our cultural, political, and spiritual dialog is not it. What we're witnessing doesn't advance anyone's point of view, nor does it advance truth. What it actually achieves is to entrench those of differing perspectives yet deeper into them. To say it diplomatically, argumentation is counterproductive. To say it more bluntly, it is stupid to argue indignantly for *A* over *B*, when it only makes *B* proponents believe *B* yet more rigidly. Anger is the *worst* possible strategy to bring anyone over the fence to one's cause—*whatever* that cause may be.

But though it does no good, we *love* to argue and debate. It is in our blood. To preserve grace in silence, as Thomas à Kempis* phrases it, is odious to the hot-blooded American spirit. Argumentation does, however, produce one significant result. It exposes immaturity.

Anger—The Life Blood of Political Discourse

"How can you support abortion—it is murder!" cry pro-life advocates. Their venom toward abortion advocates (so-called pro-choice) is as conspicuously contrary to what Jesus taught in the Sermon on the Mount ("every one who is angry with his brother shall be liable to judgment") as the "Do not kill" from the Ten Commandments they quote. According to Jesus, it will also be the angry pro-lifers, not only the pro-abortionists, who are liable to the fire of hell. The above words from Matthew 5:22 are unequivocal.

This does not imply that abortion is good or right or that they are wrong on the issue itself. That's another debate altogether. It's their anger-laced strategy that is wrong.

In arguing passionately for what they consider their righteous cause, they disobey one of the Lord's most fundamental commands. The hypocrisy is brazen and transparent. *Hypocrisy* is a hard word. I don't offer it judgmentally. I use it in its technical sense—espousing one thing (claiming to follow Jesus) and doing another (responding in anger, which Jesus forbids).

"You voted for Trump! I can't believe it! The man is corrupt, immoral, and a fool! Anyone who supported him is just as bad!" The hatred toward the former president is so rancorous and irrational that it continues to poison the national bloodstream years after his election. Far worse, it is a hatred that is transferred to anyone who speaks a kind word about him.

This doesn't imply that Mr. Trump was a good or a bad man or should or shouldn't have been elected president or that his adversaries

---

* Thomas à Kempis is author of the fifteenth-century classic *The Imitation of Christ.*

are wrong on the issue of his character. That is another debate altogether. It's their anger-laced acrimony that is wrong.

In arguing vehemently for what Trump-haters consider *their* righteous cause, they too set themselves against the entire spirit of the Sermon on the Mount. Their hypocrisy is equally transparent. Another hard word offered in as kindly a spirit as I am able to phrase it. How is their rancor somehow a loftier form of unvirtue than what they accuse Mr. Trump of?

Anti-abortionists *and* anti-Trumpers, liberals *and* conservatives, traditionalists *and* progressives, Republicans *and* Democrats are all guilty of the unvirtue of anger.

Bitter antagonism is pointless anyway. It convinces no one.

Many Virtues—One Antidote to Anger

There are different kinds of virtues—spiritual, moral, ethical, relational, intellectual. In all these, anger toward those of differing beliefs shuts down dialog, closes minds, and poisons relationships. Hostility kills the universal brotherhood of humanity.

Clearly not all those reading these words identify as Christians. But many scriptures are of universal application whether or not one subscribes to the entirety of the Christian message. The above passage from the Sermon on the Mount is one of these. Another is found in Romans 12:18: "If possible, so far as it depends upon you, live peaceably with all." The simplicity of this injunction is formidable in its utter practicality. Every one of us faces the opportunity to live by this straightforward rule of life a dozen times a day.

Christians and atheists alike are *supposed* to live peaceably with others. Not just because Paul wrote those words to the Romans two thousand years ago, but because peaceability is a virtue woven into the moral fabric of life. Living peaceably with others is a *good* thing.

How, then, can we live peaceably in America's toxic environment? How can we get along and exchange ideas in the midst of differences that are inevitable and that both sides of disputatious issues take very seriously? And how can we do so in ways that *foster* dialog, *open* minds, and promote *healthy* relationships?

The answer lies in a series of common-sense relational and intellectual virtues: kindness, courtesy, gentleness, sympathy, graciousness—nothing more nor less than being *nice*. These all come under what we might call the virtue of *civility*.

It is possible to disagree and still be respectful.

It is possible to think another wrong and treat him or her with kindness.

It is possible to discuss differences without raising one's voice.

It is possible to engage about differing political positions or spiritual beliefs or cultural ethics in a friendly and courteous spirit.

It costs nothing to be polite, amiable, diplomatic, gracious, and soft spoken.

Civility is *always* possible.

Returning to the point that is obvious from our experience yet is remarkably so little heeded, impassioned argumentation is not merely unvirtuous; it closes ears and serves no end but to feed the immature obsession to tell others where they are wrong. Civility is not only virtuous; it's the only approach by which others *might* be encouraged to listen to what you have to say.

Anger is demeaning to the universal humanity. That may not mean a great deal to others, but it means the world to me. The common humanity of God's family weighs infinitely more than any so-called temporal issue upon which you and I may disagree.

George MacDonald spoke powerfully of the universal humanity in two sermons entitled "Love Thy Neighbour" and "Love Thine Enemy." The titles alone point us far higher than mere civility, as important as that is. They lead us into the rarified air of the second of the greatest commandments: "Love your neighbor as yourself." MacDonald wrote, "Lies there not within the man and the woman a divine element of brotherhood, of sisterhood, a something lovely and lovable, . . . Shall that divine something . . . have no recognition from us?"[1]

You and I Will Not Cross Paths Today with Hitler

Let us not be sidetracked by the Hitler red herring. I don't know how I would have responded face-to-face with Hitler. It's a pointless question. I'm unlikely to face such a dilemma in my life and almost certainly not today. In *my* life today, I am called upon to be civil to the men and women who *do* cross my path.

The individuals we put forward to justify the righteous anger we nurse and cherish are but distractions from the imperative of civility and the higher imperative of love. Neither Trump nor Biden, Hillary or Bill, Obama or Pelosi, neither Democrat nor Republican—none of these are evil men and women. We may not care for their politics, but there are no Hitlers among them. They are our brothers and sisters of humanity. Each one possesses strengths and weaknesses, glaring flaws and immaturities and selfishness yet is also (as can be said of each of us) capable of moments of greatness. As much as those words may raise the hackles of the most stridently partisan, let him or her who is without sin cast the first stone.

We are all humans together, bound up in the complex dance of alternating self-glorification and self-relinquishment that characterizes our slow pilgrimage toward eternity.

11

INTELLECTUAL VIRTUE
the unvirtue: closed-mindedness

*When men differ in opinion, both sides ought equally to have
the advantage of being heard by the public; when Truth and Error
have fair play, the former is always an overmatch for the latter.*

— Benjamin Franklin

Practical strategies of civility are almost guaranteed to enhance dialog and open channels for mutually respectful communication. The character virtues that contribute to civility lay important foundations for effective relational interchange. Along with them, what are called "intellectual virtues" illuminate how people absorb and process information accurately.

We're not trying to formulate a persuasional strategy for winning arguments or convincing people to our point of view. Yet if we do want to be listened to and our perspectives taken seriously, these techniques may have that result.

Active Listening Vs. Pretense Listening

Foremost among the intellectual virtues is being able to listen attentively and respectfully to alternate viewpoints. What is called "active listening" paves the way for being heard ourselves. It implies far more than *pretending* to listen while waiting for a break in the conversation to pounce back in with a debative point countering what someone has said. That can be called *pretense listening* rather than *active listening*. It generally fools no one about one's motives. If you want to see wonderful examples of pretense listening, tune in to any political debate.

Active listening, and the practices that accompany it, act as windows into the brain that contribute to the accurate reception and processing of information. It may be as simple as the well-known principle that we are more likely to believe a truth we have discovered for ourselves than if we have been pounded over the head with it, being told we *have* to believe it, that it is *wrong* not to believe it, and that we are *stupid* if we don't believe it.

If we want information and ideas to be received accurately, the hearts and minds of our hearers have to be opened by our *own* example of genuine, humble, *listening* civility. Listening graciously doesn't necessarily imply agreement but will convey respectful civility in discourse. In handling divisive issues, we have to give people room to think for themselves. This is another means of practicing the golden rule—doing as we would be done by. I want the freedom to think for *myself*. I don't want to be bludgeoned over the head with another's opinions. It's only logical that I should give others the same freedom, treating them in discussion as I want to be treated.

Of course opinions of differing perspective may be exchanged. But *how* those differences are expressed makes all the difference in how they are received. Active listening opens brain-windows for receiving and accurately absorbing the ideas that are flowing throughout a conversation.

How Not *What* We Think

The intellectual virtues are far more than "strategies." They characterize *how* we think, not the specifics of *what* we think. Such virtues should become habits of character that reflect civility, courtesy, and respect. If we are truly interested in our fellows, we cannot feign a hypocritically humble attitude simply because it's a clever tactic to win arguments. That we have differences of outlook will be inevitable. But those differences should not obscure the brotherhood and sisterhood that exists between us.

Doing unto others as we would have them do unto us also implies not reacting to ideas too hastily or being quickly dismissive of a point of view I disagree with. When I offer my perspective on who wrote the biblical book of Hebrews, say, or who should be the next president, I want *my* thoughts given weight and respect. The Golden Rule demands that I demonstrate like respect to points of view other than mine—and not respect alone, but that I make a sincere and honest effort to *understand* the mindset of those I disagree with. It's nothing more than what I expect from them. If I cannot do so and the discussion breaks down, that failure may in part be on my head.

Processing information and ideas implies an honest love for truth and fair-mindedness. Many in the political arena are more in love with their opinionated agendas than they are of truth. It is admittedly difficult to engage in constructive dialog where an honest and fair-minded love for truth is not mutual. But let us at least be honest and fair-minded in our *own* pursuit of truth, even if others are not.

Not only is active listening imperative for information to flow between those of differing perspective, so too is avoiding mindsets and habit patterns that prevent hearing others correctly and inhibit our capacity to process information wisely.

Some of these hindrances to communication include:

- assuming we have all the answers;
- forming conclusions too quickly, often without listening carefully, thus missing crucial information and making errors in our assumptions;
- isolating ourselves in echo chambers of like-mindedness in which alternate perspectives never penetrate;
- seeking input from others, from books, or the internet not to stretch our minds but to confirm our existing beliefs;
- jumping on the bandwagon of trendy ideas or those of a perceived majority; or
- not giving alternate or unfamiliar ideas a fair hearing.

Looking for Truth Above and Beyond Our Own Opinions

A term arising out of the current academic literature is *epistemic virtue*. I'm reluctant even to include such a philosophic-sounding term that would turn virtue into a subject to be studied rather than a truth to be lived. But an important principle lies embedded here that is enormously practical if we can lay hold of it.

An epistemic virtue seeks truth without being swayed by self-interest or personal feelings. All too often what we call "truth" is so grounded in our personal biases, experiences, and beliefs that they are impossible to separate. As C. S. Lewis said about the word *gentleman* being someone the speaker likes, *truth* to the opinionated individual merely means the sum total of his or her opinions.

The insight of epistemic virtue is rooted in the recognition that "truth" as well as "virtue" exists on a higher plane than one's personal perspectives and convictions. An epistemically virtuous man or woman is able to separate personal perceptions, experience, and bias and climb up in his or her thinking to a higher plane of objectivity where opinion recedes into the background. The capacity for objectivity on that higher-truth plane is the only door into what we might call *true* truth.

Another term used in this context that I find particularly fascinating is *cognitive elasticity*. It implies no lack of conviction or wishy-washiness, but the open-minded ability to move along the spectrum of ideas, objectively seeing pros and cons of perspectives along that continuum. Its opposite, its unvirtue, is *cognitive rigidity*—being so obdurately locked into one particular immovable position that any idea in either direction to the right or left is swiftly and categorically dismissed. Elasticity allows us to believe what we believe, while recognizing nuance and give-and-take throughout the vast world of ideas. Such growing elasticity of thought is obvious in each of our lives—haven't we all found ourselves saying some variation of, "I used to think, but now . . ."?

We grow. Our matrix of ideas and perspectives changes over time.

There are limits, of course. There is a point where even the most elastic of rubber bands break. Though the continuum between the two may be wide (wide for some issues, more black and white for others), neither must we lose sight of the fact that at the two far-separated extremes of the spectrum lie *truth* and *falsehood*.

Thought-Virtues and Character-Virtues— A Tapestry of Personhood

It is natural to come at the word *virtue* through the lens of morality, ethics, and character. But the intellectual virtues are enormously important in opening us to the recognition that there are virtuous ways to *think*. There exist not only virtues of *behavior* but also virtues of *thought*. The thought-virtues, in combination with the character-virtues, act as the warp and woof upon which the entire tapestry of personhood—growth, insight, maturity, wisdom, relationships, and spirituality—is woven. It is out of this expansive tapestry that our views, outlook, and our perspective of truth emerges.

Intellectual virtues may be as important in the relational exchange of ideas as what we might call spiritual virtues. Such qualities as honesty, thoughtfulness, humility, curiosity, attentiveness to the feelings of others, self-awareness (including being aware of one's own assumptions and the potential that we can be mistaken), the maturity to objectively weigh different points of view, and charitably interpreting another's motives as sincere—these all transcend spiritual orientation. It is a "spiritual" virtue to be honest and humble, yet no less are these intellectually virtuous qualities of human character. On a more personal and human level, they inform how we relate to people all day long.

It may not *always* be possible to exhibit every intellectual virtue, especially when confronted with passionate political partisans. But if these define who *we* are, we can always try.

12

DECISIVENESS
the unvirtue: vacillation

The opposite for courage is not cowardice, it is conformity.
Even a dead fish can go with the flow.
— Jim Hightower

For some the previous chapter on intellectual virtue may have seemed taken from a college textbook, with little bearing on these cultural issues we are considering. As recommended earlier in the discussion of absolutes, I hope you won't make that judgment too quickly. In fact, the intellectual virtues have everything to do with today's cultural issues. It is those principles that influence how we think and how we assess ideas.

The war that is coming is an *idea* war. Those who are not shrewd, attentive, wise, alert, *implicational* thinkers will be among that war's first casualties.

The ideological civil war will resemble America's first civil war. The right–wrong divide won't be as straightforward as Great Britain and the United States taking up arms against Hitler's Nazism. The arguments will be multidimensional and, because they will take place within the American family, will be all the more passionate, bitter, and divisive.

Christianity Vs. the World

Without being either too simplistic or too spiritual, in its simplest terms, for Christians, this ideological war will reduce to nothing less than *Christianity vs. the World.*

The "world" in the scriptural sense, as Jesus and Paul used the word:

- "'Woe to the world for temptations to sin!'" (Matthew 18:7a).
- "'If the world hates you, know that it has hated me before it hated you. If you were of the world, the world would love its own; but because you are not of the world, but I chose you out of the world, therefore the world hates you'" (John 15:18–19).
- "He will convince the world concerning sin" (John 16:8b).
- "'My kingship is not of this world'" (John 18:36a).
- "Do not be conformed to this world" (Romans 12:2a).
- "The wisdom of this world is folly with God" (1 Corinthians 3:19a).

Traditionalism Vs. Progressivism

That said, however, to the point made earlier, it may not always resemble a "religious" conflict. For serious Christians, it will indeed be that—truth vs. falsehood, the Bible vs. secularism, Christianity vs. the world.

For nonreligious but conservative and traditional-values Americans, however, it will be a political and cultural conflict. Though their motives may be different, the two conservative-leaning groups will find themselves allies on the side of similar principles.

The example of the English Civil War (1642–51) is significant in this regard. Its loyalties were even more confusing than those of the American Civil War. In extremely simplistic terms, there was a strong *political* component and an equally strong *religious* component. Once again, the *past* leads us into an understanding of the *present*. Seventeenth-century Britain was literally torn apart in every way from its

Civil War—and those who do not discern the signs of the times and learn from history are doomed to repeat it.

Politically, it was King vs. Parliament. Religiously it was Anglicanism vs. Puritanism. Culturally, it was Rich vs. Poor.

The chief characters in the drama were Anglican King Charles and Puritan Oliver Cromwell, a parliamentarian. The country was divided along both political and religious lines that did not always align themselves as might have been expected. Not all Anglicans supported the king. Not all supporters of either the king or parliament had religious motives. The oppressed poor were spread throughout both sides. Loyalties were all over the map.

We observe exactly this in the United States. History always repeats.

Pro Trump: Many Christian men and women voted for Donald Trump in 2016, though they may have objected to aspects of his character, because they felt he most accurately supported a general Christian worldview. Others voted for him with no thought of religious considerations but because they felt he supported the traditional values of the country. Others simply because he was outspokenly pro-America.

Anti-Trump: Other Christians did not vote for him because they felt his character and behavior did *not* reflect Christlikeness. Other secularists did not vote for him because of his opposition to the liberal and progressive agenda of the Left. Still others who were more globalist in orientation saw danger is his pro-America nationalism.

Both Christians and non-Christians banned together—for their own distinct reasons—on *both* sides. Some cast their votes from spiritual motives; others voted politically and culturally.

Parallels can be seen in the election of 1980. Christians voted for Jimmy Carter specifically *because* he was an avowed born-again Christian. Other Christians voted for Ronald Reagan because they felt his conservative political perspectives were more in keeping with what they felt would be best for the country.

Again, some voted religiously; others voted culturally and politically.

A Complex Mix of Priorities and Loyalties

To amplify the battle line further, then, the coming ideological conflict may resemble:

> Modernists, Progressives, and Liberals . . .
>   (who generally hold the values, standards, perspectives, lifestyles, morals, worldview, and cultural ethics prevalent in and accepted, endorsed, and advocated by the world's culture and outlook and by those sharing those priorities—in political and cultural terms—of a *liberal and progressive* perspective)

> vs.

> Traditionalists, Conservatives, and Christians . . .
>   (who generally hold to the values, standards, perspectives, lifestyles, morals, worldview, marriage and family orientation and order, and ethics taught in the Judeo-Christian tradition and generally practiced by dedicated men, women, and families ordering their lives to the best of their fallible human capability according to the precepts of *Christianity* and by those without specific religious orientation whose conservative cultural outlook and values are rooted in the *traditional perspectives* of America's past).

Obviously glaring caveats and loopholes exist on both sides. What about where the practices of the world and the teachings of Christianity intersect? What about those affirming themselves Christians but living worldly lifestyles? And the age-old favorite by which objectors love to attack Christianity: What about so-called good and honorable secularists who may be living the Golden Rule more consistently than hypocritical Christians?

These are not insignificant questions. They deserve answers. But those discussions are best left for another time and place. They are not germane to the primary point of this chapter.

Reflecting the unspoken alliance of shared values that will become increasingly apparent:

- *Traditional American values and progressivism are incompatible.* The values, standards, morals, and lifestyles advocated by progressivism are in conflict with those of traditional historic America, not necessarily based on a rigidly literalist reading of the Constitution or the intent of the Founders but on the overriding theme and moral religious and political worldview upon which the fabric of the nation was established, which is clearly contrary to the relativism of modern culture.
- *Christianity and secular worldliness are incompatible.* The values, standards, morals, and lifestyles of the world are in conflict with those of scriptural Christianity, not necessarily based on a rigidly literalist reading of the Bible but on its overriding theme and message, which is clearly contrary to the relativism of modern culture.

These two groupings of incompatibility are obvious to those attentive to the signs of the times and to anyone who has been paying attention to the changes that have taken place in American society and culture over the past two or three decades.

What we have witnessed is only the beginning. The conflict between the world and Christianity and between traditionalism and progressivism will continue to grow in acrimony and bitterness from the Left until outright war is finally declared against those who continue to resist progressivism's relentless advance.

A Line in the Sand

Which camp within the expanding constituencies of progressivism will precipitate the conflict and openly voice the hatred that has been seething within those constituencies for years?

Though it has already said this in a thousand subtle ways, at some point progressivism will come out and openly and militantly declare to the world something along the lines of:

Judeo-Christian values no longer represent the people or future direction of America. Historic Christianity is based on a litany of superstitions and myths. The history of America is rooted in a culture of white supremacy and privilege that was responsible for slavery and continues to feed bigotry, racism, and backward thinking. The worldview of traditional America must be cast on the dung heap of history as are all failed systems. Likewise, Christianity must be put to death in America once and for all as a white belief system based in untruths and responsible for the oppression, ignorance, and judgmentalism of that history.

Or will a silent resolution arise from the Right among varying constituencies and finally say, "Enough!" Will Christians from across the spectrum (Catholics, evangelicals, Orthodox, Pentecostals, Baptists, and dedicated men and women from throughout Christendom) ban together with great numbers of traditional-thinking and conservative, though not particularly religious, Americans to declare:

We stand by and affirm the historic values of the United States and the scriptural precepts, virtues, and family order of Christianity. We will no longer pretend to agree with the cultural changes being forced upon us by progressivism and the falsehoods of the world. The agenda of anti-white, anti-male, anti-Christian, anti-marriage, anti-family, anti-law, anti-Constitution, and anti-truth is based on an emperor of progressivism wearing no clothes, a progressivism rooted in a series of lies against goodness and truth. We will go along with this deception no longer. We determine that our nation will not be overrun by these falsehoods.

The outbreak may thus closely resemble the English Civil War, with religious and secular motives all over the place on both sides that are almost impossible to disentangle.

Again, these are simplistic generalizations to characterize opposing perspectives. Neither Christianity nor secularism is one dimensional. Many secularists live by Christian principles, just as millions of Christians hold values and live lifestyles indistinguishable from worldly secularists. The millions of "Christian" women who support, vote in favor of, and consider abortion their right and the men who encourage them and support abortion to absolve themselves of their own accountability in careless sexual conduct are all the example we need of how thoroughly secularism has invaded Christendom and how self-motivated personal desire justifies the most blatant hypocrisy.

The many available red herrings must not distract us. In admittedly sweeping terms, these "sides" will increasingly come into focus. While at present there may be much fluid overlap, the priorities and perspectives of the divergent worldviews will sharpen in coming years until it becomes impossible to sit on the fence. Vacillation will be impossible. The times and issues will demand decisiveness.

Except for the most indecisive and apathetic, everyone will eventually find themselves on one side or the other. Those who think they can avoid having to make that difficult decision, and continue unthinkingly going with the flow, *have* made their decision.

The "flow" is the world. Going with the flow is simply another way of giving in and conforming to progressivism's agenda.

That is never Christ's way.

13

SPIRITUAL VIRTUE
the unvirtue: permissiveness

*If I profess with the loudest voice and clearest exposition every portion
of the truth of God except precisely that little point which the world and
the Devil are at the moment attacking, I am not confessing Christ,
however boldly I may be professing Christ. Where the battle rages, there
the loyalty of the soldier is proved, and to be steady on all the battlefield
besides, is mere flight and disgrace if he flinches at that point.*

— Martin Luther

My wife and I recently watched a movie on the attempted assassination of Adolf Hitler. In the aftermath of its failure, as the conspirators were being rounded up, the stark question was put to each, "Are you for Hitler or against him?"

It was not an idle question. Many indeed had the courage to answer, "Against." They were immediately led to a waiting firing squad.

Yea or Nay

Every American may one day have to face a scenario similar to the one above. The firing squad may not be part of it, but there are many nonphysical ways to kill those who do not go along with the majority. As we have seen, the question may be posed in either spiritual or cultural terms:

"Are you for the world and its values, perspectives, lifestyles, and ethics, or are you for Christianity and what it stands for?"
- Are you for the world or against it?

"Are you for the perspectives, lifestyles, and ethics of cultural and political progressivism, or are you for the values of traditional America and what they stand for?"
- Are you for progressivism or against it?

Right now, as the second quarter of the twenty-first century approaches, middle ground still exists between the *for* and *against*. Millions of Americans are sitting on the fence between them, living in the illusion that they can forestall a "yea" or "nay," that they can comingle the world's values, priorities, lifestyles, and ethics with their Christian and traditional beliefs. They think they can silently retain their love of America's traditional marriage, family, and other values, and their belief in American exceptionalism without having to openly reject the progressive cultural changes inundating the world around them.

Such fence-sitting will not be possible indefinitely. Issues are emerging that will divide people in myriad ways.

Eventually a yea or nay will be demanded by the aggressive and belligerent politically progressive Left and its foot-soldier ranks of militant LGBTQ, and feminist rights advocates, and BLM and Antifa Gestapo.

At first glance it may appear that this is a liberal vs. conservative, Christian vs. secularist, Republican vs. Democrat divide. That is not the case. In some ways it occasionally resembles that. But in other respects it probes much deeper into the national psyche. Those labels do not approach the core issues that are at stake. The ideological war will overleap such superficial identifications.

It will be far more complicated than a political election between Carter and Reagan, Bush and Gore, Trump and Biden, and whomever it might be in future elections. Those are binary distinctions. There are Christian progressives and Christian conservatives, just as there are progressive atheists and conservative atheists. The coming war will be nothing like a political election.

The divide plumbs deeper than politics, deeper even than religious beliefs, to the fundamental soul and center of human personhood and to the essence of what kind of country America is and should be—and what kind of men and women each of its three hundred million plus people wants to be.

Spiritual Virtue—Christianity's Most Powerful Weapon and Deepest Strength

Knowing that an ideological civil war will eventually break into the open, the central question becomes, How should traditional Americans and Christians prepare for it?

The entire point of this book is *virtue*. To frame the ideological conflict around virtue may seem naïve and simplistic. I am convinced, however, that virtue, personal and spiritual and national, is the most credible means of preparation possible.

- Moses challenged the Israelites, "Be strong and of good courage" (Deuteronomy 31:7a). *Virtue* lies at root in that challenge.
- The apostle Paul also exhorted, "Whatever things are true, whatever things are noble, whatever things are just, whatever things are pure, whatever things are lovely, whatever things are of good report, if there is any *virtue* . . . meditate on these things" (Philippians 4:8 NKJV, italics added).
- And the disciple Peter adds, "His divine power has given to us all things that pertain to life and godliness, through the knowledge of Him who called us by glory and *virtue*" (2 Peter 1:3 NKJV, italics added). "[M]ake every effort to supplement your faith with *virtue*" (2 Peter 1:5, italics added).

Virtue may not be capable of *winning* the ideological war over the world's perspectives. The world will always be the world. Following these biblical principles and exhortations, however, may be the only means possible of strengthening the internal fabric of America and Christianity so that our nation and its spiritual heritage remain vibrant and powerful in the midst of a culture that will continue morally and ethically to decline into nothing less than narcissistic hedonism.

Virtue probes deep into the marrow of what kind of people we are and want to be. It is in that center of being-ness that Christians and concerned Americans must summon the courage to resist the world's values, perspectives, lifestyles, and ethics—within the integrity of their own hearts and minds.

Yet in twenty-first-century America, all the virtues, including *virtue* itself, are on the endangered list. Progressivism scoffs at the idea of virtue as we are attempting to understand it. Progressivism lauds unvirtue as virtuous, permissiveness as enlightenment rather than weakness, and calls traditional goodness backward and bigoted. "Ethics" used to be taught in school. How can it be taught now when the virtues that undergird the very notion of ethical behavior are either endangered or already dead?

If the soul of America's individual men and women is to be saved, *true* virtue must be reclaimed.

The only effective preparation for the ideological war will take place within the hearts and minds of those men and women determined to be a virtuous people, standing strong and of good courage against progressivism's lies. A virtuous people will not necessarily convince the world of its lies. But good and virtuous and honorable men and women can stand strong within themselves so that those lies do not get inside *them*.

Doctrine and theology will not accomplish that. Sermons will not accomplish it. Arguments and apologetics will not accomplish it. The Four Laws will not accomplish it.* Debating politics will not accomplish it. Winning arguments about contemporary issues will not accomplish it. Electing one president or congress or governor over another will not accomplish it.

---

* Bill Bright wrote the *Four Spiritual Laws*—a Christian salvationary pamphlet/tract that came into widespread use during the Jesus movement in the late 1960s and 1970s.

Only the combined personal spiritual virtues that produce character and integrity will accomplish it.

The battle thus becomes not to change the world to Christianity. History and the Bible make clear that will never happen. Argument and persuasion will have no effect on the falsehoods of our time.

The battle is entirely an individual one. It is to keep my *own* values, perspectives, lifestyle, and ethics from being diluted with those of the world's failing and disintegrating culture.

Virtue—America's Most Powerful Weapon and Deepest Strength

Virtue, goodness, kindness, respect, graciousness—these are not exclusively spiritual qualities. Of course they are taught at the heart of Christianity. But they are qualities of personhood that, in one sense, are independent of belief. Goodness is not the special purview of Christianity. Goodness is the special purview of *humanity*. Or is supposed to be.

Virtue is thus also the most powerful tool to reclaim America's traditional values and core principles for those whose objection to the tidal wave of progressive changes is not primarily religious but cultural, personal, political, and historical.

The coming ideological civil war will be a battle for the heart and soul of the United States of America, for its families, its children, its future generations. To return to the point made at the beginning of the chapter, the yea or nay that may be put to us will not only be spiritual in nature.

It will also be:
- Are you for America's traditional values, perspectives, and ethics or against them?

Even more chilling:
- Are you for the Secular Replacement Nation or against it?

Whoever does not wholeheartedly give the correct answers that progressivism will demand with increasing arrogance, with fire in its eyes, will be made into the enemy.

The battle thus becomes an internal one within traditional America and within Christendom—a battle to reclaim virtues progressivism ridicules as backward and outdated. We must fight the war against both "the world" and against "modernity" by strengthening the backbone and fiber of our beliefs and values as Christians *and* as Americans.

This is not only the Christian's challenge but the challenge of *all* truth-loving Americans. It is the challenge to reclaim America's national virtue against the mirage of false virtue modernity champions.

14

ATTENTIVENESS
the unvirtue: drift

The further a society drifts from the truth,
the more it will hate those that speak it.
— Selwyn Duke

The virtue of "attentiveness" illustrates how practical and necessary virtue is for honest, tradition-valuing, and truth-loving Americans. It is an imperative virtue if this nation is to strengthen itself against the falsehoods and lies of the newly anti-American and anti-Christian sentiment sweeping our land.

Attentiveness is usually among the first of the virtues to fail. By the time it goes on the endangered-virtues list, truth has already begun to fragment and crumble.

Attentiveness fails from disuse. Other virtues follow like silent dominoes. Once attentiveness wanes, those that fade after it are hardly noticed.

The virtue of attentiveness drifts toward endangerment simply because people are not paying attention. They are not students of history. They are not discerning the times. Shrugging the shoulders to downward cultural trends, their apathetic response is, "I can't do anything about them."

Slowly they adapt, looking the other way, lowering values. One by one the *unvirtues* creep into character unnoticed—relativism, indifference, lethargy, vacillation, permissiveness—until the changes no longer seem wrong.

The unvirtue of spiritual drift—which is nothing more nor less than spiritual and mental laziness—opens the door for counterfeits of truth to steal in unseen. We listen, we absorb. We leave the doors of our character-houses unlocked and unguarded. The world's values get inside and change us.

Jesus said, "Beware of the leaven of the Pharisees and Sadducees" (Matthew 16:6). Leaven works deep inside, out of sight, invisibly. It's how progressivism's values, attitudes, and priorities have transformed America so dramatically and how they have infiltrated the church until, in many respects, the church has become one with the world's methodology and outlook.

Personal Virtue

This is not a chicken-soup-for-the-soul, nostalgic look back at the good ol' days when people were more virtuous than they are today. The very word *virtue* conveys a sense of longing for some undefined quality of life that used to be more prevalent, but that is being lost in the rush and complexity of modernity.

The allure of good-old-days thinking has been a red herring for generations. More than eighty years ago, renowned Quaker author Thomas Kelly, writing about simplicity, probed straight to the heart of a problem—not merely for his own time but which also identifies the root of the virtue-crisis in our own:

> Our complex living, we say, is due to the complex world we live in . . . which give[s] us more stimulation per square hour than used to be given per square day to our grandmothers. This explanation by the *outward* order leads us to turn wistfully, in some moments, to thoughts of a quiet South Sea Island existence, or to the horse and buggy days of our great-grandparents, who went, jingle bells, jingle bells, over the crisp and ringing snow to spend the day with *their* grandparents . . . .

Complexity . . . cannot be blamed upon complexity of our environment. . . . Nor will simplification of life follow simplification of environment. . . .

We Western peoples are apt to think our great problems are external, environmental. We are not skilled in the inner life, where the real roots of our problems lie. For I would suggest that the true explanation of . . . complexity . . . is an inner one, not an outer one.[1]

There is a certain value in looking back to former times, focusing attention on attributes we would all do well to pay more attention to. If they give thought to these things at all (unfortunately a minority), most people today are more concerned about the *present* and the *future*, about where America is headed as a nation and where the loss of virtue is taking its people and its culture.

Yet how is such a concern to be addressed? Though national in a collective sense, at root virtue is individual. Virtue is chosen deep in the innermost regions of being. Virtue is determined by what kind of people we choose to be. That's an *internal* choice made a hundred times a day in our hearts and minds, choices that then translate into the *outer* world of attitudes, perspectives, behavior, and relationships.

In that sense, the rush, pace, and complexity of contemporary life has little to do with it. This is why the Thomas Kelly quote is important, pointing us where virtue originates—within the heart, mind, and will. Kelly hit the nail on the head. The roots of the virtue-crisis confronting our nation are internal. Life's complexity and pace don't cause us to make unvirtuous choices.

However, Kelly's words are chillingly ominous considering when he wrote them—at the height of the Nazi buildup to World War II. Kelly was *in* Germany in 1938. He saw firsthand where abdication from truth could lead a nation whose people had not paid attention soon enough to the loss of virtue. Kelly's letters back to America were filled with anguish and heartbreak over what Germany had allowed itself to become.

How National Virtue Is Invisibly Lost

There exists both a personal *and* a national component to virtue. It begins personally but may not end there.

Following the sequence from individual attitudes, perspectives, and behavior, the amalgamated choices of a hundred people, then a thousand, can become, in a sense, a "group virtue" or a "group evil." The lynch mobs of the old West and reconstructionist South offer terrible examples, exactly as do the BLM and Antifa violence (or, though without the same level of widespread mayhem, the Proud Boys and Oath Keepers) of recent years. Mobs turn individual virtue-drift into mass evil.

Thousands can lead to millions until an unseen tipping point is reached. Somehow a nation of probably 95 percent *good* men and women turned into Nazi Germany. Enough individual choices, all taken together, can become—if those choices produce a nation of men and women standing strong for right and truth—a *national virtue*. But the voice of drift always argues that no one person can prevent wrong. So no one *does* stand up for right and truth. Therefore, if those combined choices allow wrong and falsehood to go unchecked, they may eventually produce a *national evil*.

How many good but silent Germans did it take before the tipping point of no return was reached?

How many good but silent American politicians will continue to allow groups like BLM and Antifa to continue unchecked, under the banner of redressing past social injustices until they become America's version of Hitler's 1920s storm troopers? Nazism began with a few hundred violent racially motivated angry fanatics. Where will the racial hatred of BLM, or whatever it has morphed into, be fifteen years from now? What role will social justice, critical race theory, gender replacement, income redistribution, and the 1619 Project play in the new constitution of the Replacement Nation thirty years from now?

The Nazi movement could have been squelched, but it wasn't. The few became a thousand. Then ten thousand. Still the good silent

German people did nothing to call out the evil. Virtue drift never ends well.

It cannot be denied, Kelly's words notwithstanding, that life *is* more complex and contains greater pressures against virtue at some times than others. Germany in the 1930s was such a time, as Kelly knew firsthand. What could one individual German have done to prevent the national evil from becoming a tidal wave that would take fifty million deaths finally to extinguish? Dietrich Bonhoeffer could not stop the Nazi juggernaut. No one German could have stopped it. But a nation with enough courageous individuals and leaders and pastors and priests and teachers and businessmen and military officers and politicians dedicated soon enough to virtue *could* have stopped it.

But drifting with the current is the easiest way. When could one or two or a hundred or a thousand courageous truth-loving Germans have changed the flow of that current—in 1931, 1929, 1925?

Drifting with the current of the culture always leads *against* virtue. By 1932, it was too late. A nation of good people had given the Nazis a majority in the Reichstag. The drift away from virtue had turned into active chosen *support* for evil. Hitler did not seize the reins of government. The German people voted the Nazis into power. No one forced them to believe. They *chose* to believe the propaganda.

It could be said that most Germans in 1932 didn't know what they were doing. But a never-voiced historical truth is a sobering one: They *should* have known. They *could* have known.

But they had been drifting with the then-prevalent perspective of German culture and society for so long that they were asleep to virtue. They had forgotten how to rise up for truth in the tradition of their revered Martin Luther and his courageous, "Here I stand." They had grown virtue-lazy and inattentive when choosing their national leaders. They *wanted* Hitler. He fed a latent national arrogance that swept them all into it. By 1932, the drift of unvirtue had grown to a flood. The point of critical momentum had passed and could not be stopped.

In 1974, Aleksandr Solzhenitsyn warned the Russian people to "live not by lies." In the same way, in a major radio address two days after Hitler was named chancellor in early 1933, Dietrich Bonhoeffer in effect tried to warn the German people on a national radio broadcast of the direction their beloved country was moving.*

Yet it was already too late. They had allowed themselves to become happily deadened to virtue. Hitler had their full support. They *should* have known; they *could* have known. The warning signs were everywhere. But attentiveness was asleep.

Don't Be Such an Alarmist

There are menacing parallels in all this with America in the third millennium. Freedoms, truth, values, the meaning of marriage, family structure, the veracity of our history as a nation, and, undergirding them all, *virtue*—true virtue—are being gradually and systematically suppressed in the name of progress. The greater good, says progressivism, demands it.

And similarly, men and women around us are *choosing* to vote the lies of progressivism into power. Neither do many of them know what they are doing (though a startling number know exactly what they are doing, which is an even more worrisome concern). What will be the future unintended consequences of their votes? We cannot see that future anymore than the Germans who voted Hitler into power in 1932 could see the atrocities that lay in the future. Nonetheless, those atrocities were on their heads.

But like the Germans of the 1930s, they *should* know. The soul of progressivism is not hard to discern. But you have to look with perceptive eyes to see it.

---

* I say "in effect" because it was not an overt warning specifically against the Nazis. But the underlying message was impossible to mistake. The topic of his address was on the then-popular concept of "The Führer Principle," in which Bonhoeffer warned about a "leader" (*führer*) rising above the authority of law. Though he did not specifically mention Hitler, a battle line was clearly drawn. His speech was cut off and never completed. Speculation has traditionally blamed the Nazis though this was never substantiated. The text of the speech was later published in the conservative newspaper *Kreuzzeitung*.

The foundations of our country are eroding before our eyes. The vast majority of Americans appear unconcerned. Most are not looking perceptively either toward the past *or* the future. Closing their eyes to the new forms of censorship being imposed, to the gradual new "interpretations" being given to the Bill of Rights, to the widespread acceptance by various political groups of the violence and looting in our streets, to the redefinition of marriage, to the horrifying indoctrination of our children, to the fragmentation of the nuclear family,* they take strange comfort in the assumption that no S.S. storm troopers or Gestapo are in our midst. America will never produce a Hitler, they say. They are not looking deep into the soul of progressivism to perceive the parallels.

There will never be outright censorship of free speech or freedom of religion. Not here. Not in America. These things could *never* happen. We are a good, kind, progressive, peace-loving, accepting people. Why all this talk about a coming war?

Sure we have ideological differences. But *war* is too strong a term. Don't be an alarmist.

No one is calling Dietrich Bonhoeffer an alarmist now. Those who say it could never go so far in America have likely never heard of Dietrich Bonhoeffer. Neither do they know their German history. If they did, it would tell them all they need to know about the virtue of *attentiveness*, and the peril of cultural, moral, societal, and political *drift*. Bad things happen when people stop paying attention.

Is this alarmist thinking?

Perhaps the parallel between 1920s Germany and 2020s America will fall on deaf ears. The forces and pressures in our culture exerting influences away from virtue, objectors will insist, are trivial compared with the blatant evils of Nazism. Who but a fanatical signboard preacher would even think a parallel exists?

One of the greatest ironies in this parallel is that the cultural Left uses it, too, with the absurd contention that it is actually American

---

* Even the "nuclear family" is a fragmentation of the biblical "family," which was multigenerational.

and Christian traditionalism that should be likened to 1930s Germany. The Left hides its *own* Nazi-like tactics behind a laughably inverted accusation.

It is the propaganda of flip-flopping its own tactics. But the placid unthinking masses swallow it, somehow accepting the misinformation they are fed, that to stand for virtue and traditional values is tantamount to killing Jews in gas chambers.

Such is the effectiveness of the Left's media-driven propaganda machine. Donald Trump became their convenient Hitler parallel, and his supporters the unthinking German masses. All this cleverly hid the sobering fact that progressivism's tactics come straight out of the Nazi playbook. President Trump served as the ideal straw man for the deception.

No one ever knows exactly where loss of virtue will lead. It always comes in miniscule ways. We hardly notice. We accustom ourselves to the drift away from virtue, even to progressivism's redefinition of what comprises virtue.

That virtue is dying around us in different ways than it did in Nazi Germany or seventeenth-century England does not mitigate the peril. America's future may not resemble anything we have seen before or can predict. But we can be certain of one thing: when true virtue dies in a nation, bad things result.

15

DILIGENCE
the unvirtue: laziness

What a terrible era in which idiots govern the blind.
— William Shakespeare, *Julius Caesar*

Diligence is usually associated with work—faithful commitment to one's duties. There is another element intrinsic to diligence that can be described as faithfulness in the details, being attentive to the small things, the finer points which might never be seen. Most of us overlook these aspects of life for exactly that reason—no one will see them. The diligent man or woman is faithful to them anyway. Duty was mentioned in a footnote earlier. The virtue of "doing one's duty" is bound up in the virtue—so evident in the biblical book of Proverbs—of diligence.

This detail-diligence of duty is nowhere more important than in personal character—virtue out of sight. Thomas à Kempis pinpoints it with precision in just three words: *Avoid small faults.*

That's where virtue grows. In life's out-of-the-way corners.

Who Cares?

The virtue erosion around us is easy to overlook. It's tame. The impact on character isn't quickly seen. The details of the erosion go unnoticed. The corners of life remain neglected.

It takes personal diligence to care about the hidden places. It's easier to be lazy, to let them slide.

Who cares if every movie is filled with unseemly language and bedroom scenes, normalizing profanity and sex in ways no one would have put up with fifty years ago? Who cares if schoolchildren are taught to be ashamed of themselves simply for being white because to be white is to be racist? Who cares if they are openly encouraged to declare themselves gay or lesbian, or even declare themselves of the opposite gender? It's nothing so terrible. Who cares if critical race theory is based on a new form of racism just as surely as slavery in the U.S. was based on past forms of racism? Who cares if America's history is rewritten and taught to school children based on outright falsehoods? Who cares if *injustice* is invisibly woven into the warp and woof of the lie going by the name "social justice"?

Is anyone diligent enough in the small virtues to say, "Enough!"

Even thirty years ago, a virtue grid in Hollywood recognized that certain things were wrong to flagrantly put on screen. Admittedly it wasn't a tight grid. Now there is no grid at all. Sex and immorality and profanity are normal. Every film or TV sit-com must have gay or trans characters. Even Hallmark has given in to the all-powerful LGBTQ lobby. Who cares if school boards and the NEA now have more influence in engendering values in America's public school children than their parents?

But hey—no big deal. No one's arresting Jews. No Gestapo is breaking into our homes at night. There's no Stalinesque gulag in Siberia awaiting transgressors. A little bad language, liberal textbooks in school, a little critical race theory, rewriting American history, prejudice against whites, some judicious lying by the media to prop up liberals and denigrate conservatives—so what?

We're too lazy to be diligent, too lazy to avoid small faults. Too lazy to pay attention to life's corners.

For want of diligence in the small things, virtue fades. It's the cultural drift. The cause: laziness.

How Long Will Christians Conform to Moral Drift?

Christians and traditional thinking Americans are complicit. They go along. They keep watching the movies and sending their children to public schools and voting for politicians who vote to fund abortions.

They vote. Babies die. But they never connect the dots. It doesn't occur to them that their lack of diligence is contributing to the erosion of virtue.

Christian men and women are producing unwanted pregnancies with unbiblical sexual conduct. Christian women are having abortions—ghastly as that sentence even is for me to write. Christian men encourage it. Christians by the millions are endorsing same-sex marriage. All I can wonder is what their so-called Christian faith means to them.

Without knowing it, by their lack of diligence to the small things of character, all these are saying yea to the question, "Are you *for* progressivism?"

Many Christians are saying yea. Many traditional Americans are saying yea. They are saying it in a thousand ways. Thus progressivism implants the lies of its agenda into our minds and churches and homes and families with scarcely a whimper of protest.

That's the alarming parallel with 1920s Germany and the Soviet Union of the 1950s and 1960s. Not that BLM activists are about to be voted into a majority in Congress and then put one of their own in the White House. The parallel is that Americans are going along with society and culture. We are allowing ourselves to absorb dozens of views and perspectives that, if we stopped to think about them and set them alongside what Jesus taught, we would dismiss them in an instant. But they creep in slowly, subtly, unnoticed. We shrug our shoulders.

Hitler indoctrinated a nation to hate Jews. Good Christian Germans went along. They weren't diligent enough in the small things, so they let them slide. It began slowly—first, just notice the Jews, then suspect them, then fear them, then hate them. Ten years later

Jews were being arrested and killed in the streets. Still no one spoke up.

Progressivism is indoctrinating a nation of Americans to live by a litany of lies—lies that began small, then grew and grew until now they are lies taking over our culture. All the while good Christian Americans go along, asleep like everyone else.

Good German Christians and good American Christians drifting with the culture.

What Would Jesus Say?

We give scarcely a thought to the question: What would Jesus say if he walked into the room? Would we welcome him and invite him to sit down with a bowl of popcorn in his lap and watch the R-rated movie with our children and Christian friends? Would he sit laughing and joking with us as he watched a premarital bedroom scene or two gay men kissing or listened to the characters profaning him and his Father, not bothered because he loves them all and doesn't mind how they live or what influence they are having on the youth of an entire culture? It used to be, "Hate the sin but love the sinner." Now it's, "Pretend not to notice the sin."

When we were young, we used to ask, "If Jesus returned suddenly, would I be pleased, or embarrassed, for him to see what I am doing, what I am saying, what I am thinking, at this very moment?"

What would Jesus do if he walked into a church that proclaimed him as Savior in the middle of a same-sex wedding ceremony? Would the pastor or priest invite him to come up and give the happy couple the honor of marrying them himself?

What *would* Jesus do? Would he say, "How wonderful! Isn't the love of these two a great example of the expansiveness of the love of God?" Or would he say, "Go and sin no more."

What would George Washington, Thomas Jefferson, Abraham Lincoln, or Jesus himself think of same-sex marriage, abortion, the sex and violence we expose our children to, the video games we let our children play? What does Jesus think about the politicians we mindlessly elect who endorse unvirtue at every turn?

What does Jesus think about teachers who teach children that gender is a choice, going along with the culture because, well, what can one person do anyway? Why have Christian teachers not quit by the millions and started their own schools, rather than having to teach such lies? Why do they silently go along?

Years ago Francis Schaeffer prophetically pinpointed the church of today when he said, "There is a sad myth going around today—the myth of neutrality."[1]

Today's Christians are living within that myth every day, pretending that it is possible to be neutral toward progressivism.

If we're not paying attention and choosing well, if we listen to the voices of modernity, we will continue slowly and mindlessly drifting with the world's current. When will it have gone so far that *we* have become collaborators in the evil?

Schaeffer also said, "Tell me what the world is saying today, and I'll tell you what the church will be saying in seven years."[2] It no longer takes seven years. The church brings the world's methods and music, its priorities and values and outlook, its cultural changes, its tolerance of sin, straight in through its wide-open doors in a matter of months. How many beliefs and practices that the church abhorred two generations ago have been almost entirely normalized within Christendom? It's not just R-rated movies and loose language, it's adultery, divorce, abortion, homosexuality, relativistic truth, gay and lesbian clergy, rap music, loss of absolutes, sex outside marriage, dishonor of parents. The list goes on.

Attentive detail diligence in the church has vanished. Christians are not merely willing; they are *eager* to jump on the world's bandwagons, hungrily lapping up everything the culture tells them. When the ideological war breaks out in full fury, one cannot but wonder which side many churches will be on.

What will be the yea or nay of the church?

What Will History Say?

At what point will future historians looking back, trying to put into perspective the final death throes of the great "American experiment in democracy" and its ultimate failure—looking back at *us*—say:

- "They could have stopped it in 2008 or 2020 or 2022 or 2024 or 2026. They *should* have stopped it. But they had been drifting with the lethal perspective of societal change for so long that they were asleep to morality, virtue, and truth. They had forgotten how to stand up for right and wrong."
- "The end didn't come with guns and armed insurrection nor by political or military coup. America died from an invisible cancer that had been allowed into its bloodstream. It was a virus that severed its Christian roots and produced a virtue-lazy and inattentive populace. By 2028 it was too late—or 2035 or 2040."
- "They *could* have stopped it; they *should* have stopped it. But by then the disease was too deep into the marrow to be reversed. The ideological war was won by progressivism, and the other side never even knew war had been declared."

When will twenty-first-century America reach the tipping point when national virtue has been allowed to drift invisibly and irrevocably away?

The Replacement United States of America is coming—unless the lies are exposed.

16

AUTHENTICITY
the unvirtue: guile*

*Secular progressives tend to rearrange their bigotries
and call it righteousness.*
— Rod Dreher

In his book *Live Not by Lies*, Rod Dreher uses a term that at first glance left me scratching my head. As it has worked on my sub-conscious, however, I see how appropriate the term is in pinpointing precisely the state of affairs in which we in 2020s America find our-selves. As the ideological war gathers momentum around us, Dreher maintains that in the early years of the third millennium, we in the West, and especially in the United States, are living under a regime of *soft totalitarianism.*

Soft Totalitarianism

Classic governmental totalitarianism exerts total control over the lives of its citizens, usually militarily. This control extends to every aspect of individual life through coercion and repression. There is no individual freedom. A powerful police state enforces control. Opposing the rule

---

* *Guile* is an uncommon term today although many will recognize it from John 1:47 where, seeing Nathanael approaching, Jesus remarked that he was a man in whom was "no guile." I translate his meaning as, "Here comes a man with nothing to hide—sincere, frank, and honest—an *authentic* man." Guile is a cousin to hypocrisy, indicating shadows of character kept from view, appearing what one is not, hiding duplicitous, cunning, crafty, deceitful motives and schemes. An authentic man or woman is who he or she is, true to truth, open, transparent, integrated and whole of character and personhood.

of the all-powerful state results in prison or even execution. People adapt and learn to live under the system because they have no choice. The only alternative is constant danger, with the threat of being discovered and arrested.

Totalitarianism is dehumanizing. Those who choose to adapt do so by gradually sacrificing their own personhood on the altar of fear. They learn to call right wrong. They learn to be silent. They learn to say, "*Heil* Hitler," though they hate themselves for doing so. Eventually the words fall so easily from their lips that they no longer hate the words, or hate what saying the words has made of them. The brainwashing by *the system*, implemented by fear, has completed its work.

The soft totalitarianism of our time functions according to exactly the same principles but without the military component. The enforcement mechanism is civilian. The liberal culture of political correctness is delivered into the general culture—into homes, families, and malleable brains—by the news media, academia, and Hollywood. Your favorite college professor, the ABC or NBC anchorman or -woman you rely on, your trusted newspaper columnist, your never-miss sitcoms, your favorite movie stars and late night talk show hosts, your senator and congressman or congresswoman, your beloved president, and even your son or daughter's fifth grade teacher—they wear no arm bands or uniforms. But they are all puppets of soft totalitarianism, spreading its doctrines into every facet of life.

The control they exert does not force military compliance, but rather *thought-compliance.* You must go along with the acceptable ideas, words, attitudes, and cultural mores, or you will pay a price for your noncompliance.

You must silently agree when they say, "Heil Progress, Heil Wokeism, Heil BLM, Heil LGBTQ, Heil Women's Rights. Heil Social Justice, Heil Revisionist History, Heil Courageous Transgenders, Heil Whites Who Apologize for Being White." Down with conservatism, down with evangelicalism, down with Trump supporters, down with white racism, down with statues of America's white heroes, down with whites who don't admit they are part of systemic racism, down with all financial inequities.

More than a few go along. Tens of millions have been thoroughly indoctrinated into the new unreality. They are foot soldiers in the new order. Soft totalitarianism needs no army. The brainwashed citizenry of the religion of wokeism carries out the function free of charge. They shout, *"Sieg heil!"** with the gusto of true believers exalting in modernity's takeover of American culture and politics.

What about the millions who are fearful of saying no to the lie of revisionist history? No to wokeism? No to calling a boy "she" and a girl "he"? No to the new racism of critical race theory? And most controversial of all, no to abortion and the LBGTQ agenda?

Honest and *thinking* Americans know right from wrong. They know illogical falsehoods when they see them. What will they do?

Will they mouth their silent *heils* in spite of it, for fear of reprisals by family and friends and coworkers, fearful of the stinging attacks that will be leveled against them for being backward, ignorant, bigoted, racist, judgmental, and hateful if they even *think* about saying no?

When the question is posed in a hundred different ways, "Are you for progressivism?" will they continue silently to say yea?

Will they give in, drift with the current, sacrifice what they know to be right, relinquishing personhood until the lie has become part of them?

How many Germans would have been necessary to stop Hitler? It is one of the great enigmas of history. How many Nazis, how many ruthless Gestapo sadists, were once kind-hearted husbands and fathers who said, *"Heil,"* so many times that the lie entered the bloodstream of their thoughts and hatred took them over?

What does it take to stop a lie?

It takes *authentic* men and women who refuse to let the lie inside them, who refuse to bow to the lie, who refuse to say, *"Heil"* to the Lie.

---

* Hail victory!

Genuine Men and Women

Authenticity is one of the most urgently needed virtues of our time. It too, however, is on the endangered-virtues list. The lies of soft totalitarianism press so powerfully against us that they squeeze virtue out. Along with attentiveness, authenticity is among the first to go.

The politically correct culture of soft totalitarianism has not only created a "silent majority" (though that too) but worse—an *inauthentic* majority. A vast population of generally honorable and right-thinking men and women afraid to be themselves, afraid to say what they think, afraid to be diligent in life's corners, afraid to be genuine and honest and true. They are so fearful of reprisals they allow it to be assumed that they are among the minions of *the system* saying, "*Sieg heil*" to progressivism along with their peers.

Laying down authenticity in favor of political correctness, going along with the crowd, inevitably sacrifices a piece of freedom, a vital portion of one's humanity. True personhood slowly and inexorably dies.

The synonyms of authenticity are striking—reliable, real, accurate, trustworthy, dependable. Such qualities of character, by their very nature, stand on the side of truth. It is impossible for authenticity to sanction falsehood.

The most piercing definition of authentic, however, is this: "Genuine, faithful to the original and of undisputed origin."

Our origin, and thus our "original," is God our Father.

He created you and me in his image. Jesus is the fullness of his being in the flesh—God in the reality of manhood. Jesus is the genuine image of his Father, the one fully *authentic* Man.

We have been birthed into the same life that was in Jesus. We are reproductions of him. But unlike the art world where only one genuine original exists, in the spiritual realm, copies of the original are also genuine. I am a *genuine* part of the originating life of the universe! My origin is undisputed. My life's calling is to be a faithful image of the one Son, because I, too, am a genuine son of his Father.

Perhaps this deeply spiritual argument for authenticity will not be as meaningful to some readers as to others. I can only speak for myself, therefore, in saying that my calling is to authentically live the originating life that is in me.

Protests, guns, politics, books, elections, newspapers, arguments, debates—no external or societal methods or programs can extinguish falsehood. *Authenticity of personhood* is the only reality that can defeat a lie.

In Authenticity of Personhood, I Stand

The cross of Christ defeated the great Lie. In the small world where I live as a Christian man, my personal authenticity is all that stands between myself and the world's lies. Reminding myself that I am a genuine, though small, image of Jesus, the one true and authentic Man, I refuse the lie entrance to my mind and heart.

- I will not endorse it.
- I will not give verbal consent to it.
- I will not pretend to agree.
- I will not be untrue.
- I will not allow guile to define my personhood.
- No "*heils*" will pass my lips. No silent agreement to progressivism's lie will sprout and grow in the soil of my thoughts.

I will be faithful to myself, to Jesus, and to God the Father.
In the power of that authentic reality, I take my stand for truth.

17

HONESTY
the unvirtue: groupspeak

I'm just going to say it. We have an evil president.
We have a bad Pope. I am a son of the Church. I respect the chair of Peter
and pray for this Pope. I do not respect this President.
— Deacon Keith Fournier

Though these words by Deacon Fournier do not ring with gentleness, I quote him for one reason. He is honest. These are the words of an authentically honest man. Obviously from all that has come before, notwithstanding some of my own bold words, it is clear that I do not believe this tone will be especially useful in the ideological war. That said, as I will share in the next chapter, speaking forcefully in the public square may indeed occasionally be called for. And with authenticity in such short supply among thinking Christians and Americans in today's culture, I admire Mr. Fournier's pluck and courage.

Groupthink

The terms *newspeak* and *doublethink* were made famous in George Orwell's book *1984*. Conformity to the state was enforced by new ways of thinking and speaking. They were illogical and irrational. But in their desire to conform to the perceived majority opinion (often imaginary), the masses adopted what they were told to think and faithfully spoke the lies.

The term *groupthink* was first coined a little more than two decades after publication of the Orwell classic. To explain certain decisions of American foreign policy, notably the Vietnam War in the late 1960s, groupthink was defined as a mode of decision making in which members of a group accept a viewpoint or conclusion that represents a perceived consensus. The individuals themselves may not believe those viewpoints or even consider them optimal to achieve their goals. They may not even represent the *actual* majority opinion. Most of the group may be *against* the idea. But they go along, assuming it represents what everyone else believes. A minority and ill-advised conclusion may win the day because of a false perception and the fear to go against it. Groupthink is obviously a poor basis for decision making, death to wise and analytical thought, and numbing to individuality.*

There is little need to draw the parallel with America of the 2020s. *Groupthink* and *groupspeak* are in the very air of our times, often going by the name "political correctness" though that term is gradually fading from favor in the monthly-updated nomenclature of wokeism. Whatever it's called, we all know the kinds of things you're not supposed to say aloud.

Groupspeak is the great enemy of authenticity. Fearing to be out of step with "the group," we either mouth what is expected or say nothing. We retreat into our shells. Reality, genuineness, honesty—gone with the wind. We are too timid to be entirely and authentically honest.

Free Speech and Authentic Nonconformity

Groupspeak is simply another name for conformity. The 1972 book by I. L. Janis in which the term originated, *Victims of Groupthink: A*

---

* A corollary of groupthink is a foundation stone in Saul Alinsky's "Ten Rules for Radicals." It is the very first of the rules: "Power is not only what you have but what the enemy thinks you have." Alinsky's *Rules for Radicals* was published in 1971. Hillary Rodham was his devoted disciple. Alinsky's "Rules" form the basis for the opening scene in *The Invisible War,* the first volume in my series Tribulation Cult, the fictional companion to this book.

Psychological Study of Foreign-policy Decisions and Fiascoes, was published on the very heels of the anti-war movement, anti-government protests, and the civil unrest of the 1960s.

It was the era of Vietnam, the Beatles, Woodstock, and Watergate. Nonconformity was worn as a badge of honor by students, protesters and dissidents. *Conformity,* as personified by the "groupthink" that held the Pentagon in its grip and prolonged the Vietnam War, was the great evil. Irreverent, in-your-face, nonconformist John Lennon personified the free-thinking, anti-establishment image of the times.

The liberal Left of the sixties became radicalized precisely by militantly branding itself as *nonconformist.* Conformity was evil. Nonconformity was hip, cool, in.

Fifty years later, all this has turned upside-down. Nonconformity is now the great evil. You must *conform* to the accepted modes of expressions, vocabulary, and patterns of thought—down to Big Brother's regulation of what pronouns are now acceptable in daily use. The free-speech movement is dead. The progressive neo-Left has become the very "establishment" its predecessors hated. It rules by enforcing conformity to all the agenda points of its narrative. Its insistence that the country bow to its ideology has become more frightening than any of Richard Nixon's so-called dirty tricks. The Left despised Nixon yet has now become more ruthless and guileful than anything even imagined in the Nixon White House.

The liberalism born in the sixties has become the Orwellian all-powerful party of the fictional country Oceana. Dissent is not allowed. Big Brother, as Orwell's characters knew all too well, may be watching you. Your cell phones and televisions and computers *are* watching, listening, invading your privacy in ways no one ever imagined could occur. Orwell's fiction has become the reality of our technologically intrusive society. The free-thinking nonconformists of the sixties are now in charge of the very government it once despised. The inmates have taken over the asylum.

With conservatives increasingly banned from social media and ostracized in academia, the media, and business, where is free speech now?

Rod Dreher writes:

> The foundation of totalitarianism is an ideology made of lies. The system depends for its existence on a people's fear of challenging the lies. . . . [D]espite its superficial permissiveness, liberal democracy is degenerating into . . . soft totalitarianism . . . .
>
> Today's totalitarianism demands allegiance to a set of progressive beliefs, many of which are incompatible with logic—and certainly with Christianity. . . .
>
> [W]e are not likely to face widespread rioting and armed insurrection. . . . But that doesn't mean we aren't ripe for a new and different form of totalitarianism . . . a state in which nothing can be permitted to exist that contradicts a society's ruling ideology.[1]

Former judge Keith Alber wrote about reading in a 1954 collegiate political science textbook an outline for some of the steps necessary to overturn a democracy.[2] Among them were:

- Divide the nation philosophically.
- Foment racial strife.
- Work to cause distrust of police authority.
- Swarm the nation's borders indiscriminately.
- Weaken the military.
- Continually increase taxation.
- Encourage civil rioting.
- Lessen accountability for crime.
- Control election outcomes.
- Control the media.

The woke state of progressivism is well on its way. I make it nine and a half out of ten.

Scriptural Nonconformity That Will Change the World

Again Rod Dreher writes:

> Christians today must understand that, fundamentally, they aren't resisting a different politics but rather what is effectively a rival religion. . . .
>
> Many conservatives today fail to grasp the gravity of this threat, dismissing it as mere "political correctness" . . . . [T]hey are afraid to resist, because they are confident that no one will join them or defend them. . . .
>
> Under the emerging tyranny of wokeness, conservatives, including conservative Christians . . . convince themselves that they can live honestly within woke systems by outwardly conforming and learning how to adapt their convictions to the new order.[3]

For Christians, more is at stake than politics. Christians are *commanded* not to go along with groupthink or groupspeak. We are commanded to be *spiritual nonconformists.* Paul's words in Romans 12:2 are unambiguous: "Do not be conformed to this world."

Christian nonconformity is not that of the picketer, rioter, rock thrower, flag burner, debater, abortion clinic protester, or outspoken blogger. It is the nonconformity that refuses to go along with the groupspeak and groupthink of a world intoxicated in the illusion of the new woke unreality.

Some may consider it their duty and calling to visibly, vocally, and perhaps publicly express their traditional and Christian, though now nonconformist, convictions. Some may do so anonymously. It may be that still others will not choose outward forums in which to make their stand for truth. These may live their authenticity more privately among those with whom they are in close relationship.

But the call to guileless, honest, authenticity of personhood is universal.

Nor is it *primarily* public but private. It may lead to more public expressions for some than others. But fundamentally the virtues of *attentiveness*, *authenticity*, and *honesty* begin within. That is where the initial and most important battle for truth is birthed. It is where the ideological war will be won or lost. It is within our hearts that we remain true to ourselves.

Attentive to truth, refusing to drift with the world's current, honest authenticity of personhood is the most powerful weapon to defend truth. Dietrich Bonhoeffer and Aleksandr Solzhenitsyn and Martin Luther will never be forgotten. They were attentive, authentic, honest men who refused to give in to the lies of the ideological conflicts of their times.

Those who may disagree with me are not my primary responsibility.

- *I am the one* who must not be seduced by the lies.
- *I am the one* who must remain attentive.
- *I am the one* who must not drift with the world's current.
- *I am the one* exhorted to live not by lies.
- *I am the one* called to authenticity of personhood.
- *I am the one* called to honesty as a man, a Christian, and an American.

I am not called to convince others not to live by the world's lies *but not to embrace the lies myself.* The world will not care what I say. This is a call to arms to Americans and Christians to recapture virtue where it has faded—then to stand as attentive, honest, and authentic men and women, living *in* virtue and, as we are led, defending virtue. Most of all within our own hearts.

For myself, I determine never to convey that I endorse the lies. Beyond that, I do not perceive it my job to convince or argue or persuade. Die-hard progressives and wokeists cannot be convinced. My responsibility is to live truth *myself.*

More important than not conforming to the world, I am commanded not to judge, get angry, dispute, argue, and above all to love. That includes loving and forgiving my enemies. I view no brother or sister of humanity as an *enemy* as such, certainly not one merely holding a viewpoint I may consider unfounded and contrary to truth.

Many in today's world, however, are deceived by the lies of our culture. In that sense, they have made themselves enemies of truth. The other side of the coin is more frightening. Strident progressives *do* consider traditional Americans and conservative Christians enemies. I must not be oblivious to the fact that they will consider me *their* enemy.

Still, my calling is not to persuade or debate. Speaking in defense of truth merely to persuade or convince may not rise to the level of love. Jesus defeated the great Lie by love.

18

RESPECT
the unvirtue: scorn

Wrong does not cease to be wrong because the majority share in it.
— Leo Tolstoy

An important potential misperception must be addressed here. Terms like *sympathy*, *humility*, *courtesy*, *empathy*, a *listening spirit*, and all the other intellectual virtues discussed in chapter 10 can easily be misconstrued. These are clearly expressions of tolerance, acceptance, and kindness. It may be that they will be misunderstood as referring to *ideas*, as if being "civil" means being accepting, tolerant, courteous, and empathetic toward idea *X* when I consider idea *X* false. Latching onto this incorrect conclusion provides easy justification for rejecting the notion of kindness and civility altogether. How can I be respectful toward an idea I believe is wrong?

Individuals and Ideas—Keeping the Distinction Clear

Individuals and *ideas* must be kept separate in our hearts and minds. Otherwise we will drift into bias, intolerance, condescension, and judgmentalism toward the *people* we are commanded to love and treat with respect and kindness.

If we are paying attention, thinking clearly and rationally, and not allowing our emotions to run away with us, if we are paying heed to avoid the hindrances to communication mentioned in light of intellectual virtue, our response to individuals and ideas will be different. We cannot approach the two in the same way. Even when an idea is held so zealously by an individual that for all practical purposes it defines him, when he or she is so taken over by the idea that their personal character *is* the idea, we must yet seek the invisible dividing line. We must discover the *man* or *woman* himself or herself apart from whatever ideas consume them.

That man or woman—the essential child of God who is *not* defined by the ideas they hold—is worthy and deserving of our kindness and respect.

It cannot be said that the ideas we hold have *nothing* to do with the men and women we are. Practically speaking, our beliefs and perspectives *are* bound up in the mix of what defines personhood. For the purposes of living virtuously beside and toward our fellows, however, ideas are not merely secondary; they do not enter into the civility equation in any way whatever.

Terms like *empathy* and *elasticity* are therefore easy to misunderstand. They might appear to imply a sympathetic response to another's perspectives and viewpoints. Keeping the distinction clear, however, enables us to demonstrate respect toward *individuals*—trying to feel and see through their eyes, attempting to walk in his or her shoes, listening with understanding and compassion to "where they are coming from."

This may be different than how we would respond to the ideas they hold. Respect requires no alignment of beliefs or viewpoints. It only requires a heart of love and a spirit of kindness. There may occasionally come times when elasticity in our response to ideas is called for. Or there may *not*. We may disagree wholeheartedly with certain ideas. But no one with whom we interact in *any* circumstance should mistake that a caring and compassionate heart lies deeper within us than idea-disagreements.

Finding the Dividing Line

In the political sphere, the blurring of lines between ideas and individuals is almost total. Hillary Clinton's labeling of her opposition's supporters as a "basket of deplorables" has entered the vernacular as a metaphor for demeaning the worth, dignity, and intellect of those with whom we disagree. She was using this tactic long before she ran for president, showing contempt for stay-at-home-women with her sarcastic, "I could have stayed home and baked cookies."[1]

President Obama was more polished and subtle with his scorn toward what he, as the standard-bearer of progressivism in the new millennium, considered the unenlightened. Though when he blundered into speaking of Midwesterners with, "they cling to guns or religion or . . . anti-immigrant sentiment," his condescension was no less egregious.[2]

Both met their match in candidate and former President Trump. His demeaning and bombastic style was not only appalling; it was all the more embarrassing when he turned it against opponents with whom he generally agreed on the issues. At that point it served no purpose but to insult and ridicule, and revealed little more than his own immaturity of character.

Yet politics lives by this misapprehension that an individual's worth and dignity rests on his or her beliefs. The Left disparages traditionalists as unsophisticated and intellectually inferior, often tearing down their humanity on the basis of deeply held spiritual convictions. The Right condemns progressives as being void of spiritual and ethical standards because of *their* viewpoints.

I hope I can say this with grief in my heart, not the very unvirtues I am speaking against, but the basket of deplorability lives in Washington, DC, not in middle America. It is nothing less than deplorable that the engine of our nation's leadership feeds on such false presuppositions. It is all the more unforgivable when those who buck this tide, and against all odds rise to national prominence and attempt to give their opponents the dignity and respect of human brotherhood, are lambasted as simpletons and fools. In politics, humility would seem to be a liability.

There is a time to respond to ideas. Moments come in life to confront perspectives we consider wrong. There may also be a necessary component in calling out the *people* who embrace and teach those false ideas. Response to falsehoods must occasionally be strong. There are good ideas and bad ideas. Righteousness and evil coexist in the world. They are not the same. But individuals and ideas are distinct. People always come first. All men are deserving of my respect, never my scorn. That said, *people* are nevertheless accountable for the *ideas* they embrace. Evil exists both in ideas *and* in the heart of those who allow it to grow there.

No clearer example of the dividing line between the two exists than in one of the Bible's most misunderstood verses. In Mark 8:33, Jesus turned on Peter with the words, "Get behind me, Satan! For you are not on the side of God, but of men." It is easy to think Jesus was calling *Peter* Satan. This is exactly the nub of the misperception. Peter was Jesus's close friend. He loved and respected Peter with a love we can scarcely fathom. The "Satan" was the idea Peter had expressed. Jesus rebuked the *idea* not the man.

It is true that Jesus may have also been angry with Peter for allowing a false idea to take hold within him. That's where the balance becomes tricky to discern—Peter was yet accountable as a *man* for the *idea* he had let into his heart. Elsewhere we are told that Jesus was angry with the Pharisees for their hardness of heart (Mark 3:5). A hard heart may indeed be cause for righteous anger. Allowing false ideas to take root and consume one's outlook on life and God and the world is certainly cause for indignation. But Jesus understood the difference in a way we are rarely capable of. He gave his life in love for those same Pharisees, even as he was killing the evil ideas that had hardened their hearts.

The *Very* Difficult Balance

These balances are *hard*. It will be easy for critics to condemn me for being uncivil in some of my remarks. How do we assess ideas and people, and respond appropriately to both, when we *don't* have the perfect insight into the hearts of men that Jesus had?

I have been a student of human nature all my life. My writing has forced me to examine people, personalities, motives, strengths, and weaknesses. I observe real people in the same way I develop characters in my books. One cannot be a student of human nature and remain unaware of the fact that the world is made up of a few growing, wise, mature, authentic, and integritous men and women and a great many stagnant, foolish, immature, dishonest, and inauthentic people. It is not necessarily unvirtuous to recognize immaturity, foolishness, or disingenuous motives when we see them. It's how we handle our observations that determines civility or anger, respect or scorn. In the spirit of Thomas à Kempis, most of the time we are probably on solid ground to keep those observations to ourselves.

The comments I have occasionally made here about the ego and immaturity of some of our leaders, I hope, do not come across as personal attacks but, rather, as recognition of weaknesses that in some cases need to be addressed. In the recent two presidential elections, I have been aghast at the immaturities of candidates Clinton, Trump, Biden, and Harris. I confess I became angry at their childishness. I hope I say that in the same spirit with which Jesus was angry with the Pharisees.

Is it hypocritical to urge civility and respect yet speak forcefully about some of our leaders? That question pinpoints why I say these are *hard* things. Were I to meet any of the above four individuals personally, I would offer my hand and be honored for the opportunity—honored not because I necessarily respect their wisdom or integrity, but for the same reason I hope I am capable of honoring all men and women as children of God. There is not an ounce of hostile acrimony in my heart toward any of them, even as I recognize that some of the ideas they hold, and the immature examples they have set, *should* rouse thinking Americans to question why such individuals are setting America's cultural agenda in ways that erode its spiritual and ethical fabric.

How can we respectfully, civilly, graciously, and without anger recognize that a self-motivated and immature individual has adopted false ideas and life priorities; that those false ideas and priorities are causing a lack of integrity, honor, truthfulness and wisdom and are death to true character; and, if he or she is active in the public square, that those falsehoods and priorities of untruth are spreading their cancers into millions of hearts and contributing to the ruination of our nation?

If we recognize such things, when and how is it appropriate to speak them?

I don't have perfect answers to these questions. I struggle with them every day. This book is my attempt to thread that needle. Whether or not I have done so judiciously and in a kindly spirit, I will always wish I could have done better in finding the balance.

Perhaps these personal comments only muddy the water. I'm certain, however, that most readers will know exactly what I mean and will have wrestled with precisely these difficult questions.

An even more probing example of Jesus zeroing straight in on the invisible dividing line—not merely between individual and idea but between individual and *sin*—is found in John 8 where Jesus confronts the woman caught in adultery.

His, "Neither do I condemn you; go, and do not sin again" (John 8:11) is full to overflowing with application for our time. Sin exists. There are times to recognize sin while preserving respect. There may be times we recognize sin in our national leaders. Jesus respected the woman as a sister of humanity. But he equally recognized her sin of adultery. Neither do I condemn *you* (my sister whom I love), now *sin no more.*

There is a season to rebuke false ideas and even to confront sin, following Jesus's example by doing so while preserving respect for the inherent humanity of those even in whom we recognize immaturities that are damaging for our nation. It is occasionally necessary to wade into such waters but to do so with great care. We cannot approach those turbulent waters, however, until the primacy of *individual over idea* and *individual over sin* is a principle lodged as a granite foundation in our minds.

I reject altogether the examples of Hillary Clinton, Barack Obama, and Donald Trump in responding to differences of idea-viewpoint. I am not speaking of their political viewpoints but of the *unvirtue* of scorn that prevented all three from living the *virtue* of respect toward all men. They are not worthy role models. They have not upheld the dignity of the human family nor the dignity of the *American* family. Our nation was torn apart by a civil war once. Civility and respect toward the individuals who make up the *whole* American family, irrespective of the ideas they hold, may be the only thing that will prevent another.

19

COURTESY
the unvirtue: rudeness

A return to first principles in a republic is sometimes caused
by the simple virtues of one man. His good example has such an influence
that the good men strive to imitate him, and the wicked are ashamed
to lead a life so contrary to his example.

— Niccolo Machiavelli

Let me return for a moment to C. S. Lewis's statement from the first chapter: "There was no contradiction in saying that John was a liar and a gentleman."

We might imagine two responses to this fictional John. The practicality of the analogy will be increased many times if instead of "John" we think of our good Republican or Democrat friend with whom we disagree on almost everything.

I'll make it more personal yet. John is *my* liberal or conservative friend. My first imaginary response to what he has said is one of anger, finger wagging, red faced, and with eyes aflame: "John, you cad and scoundrel—you're a liar!"

Or a second alternative demonstrating the virtue of soft-spoken courtesy: "John, with all due respect, I think you might not have spoken the truth here. Could we talk about it—I'd like to know what you were thinking when you said it. I'm wondering if you might be having second thoughts?"

Responding to Differences

What does it cost to exercise intellectual virtue? Only a modicum of courtesy, humility, kindness, and a listening spirit. Tone and demeanor are everything. My friend must *feel* kindness. He must sense goodwill in my countenance and bearing. He must know I am sincere in asking for an explanation, that I genuinely want to understand his side of things.

Yet courtesy is a two-way street.

In the second instance, if John leaps from his chair and rudely cries, "How dare you accuse me of lying! You have no right! This conversation is over—get out!" then courtesy and civility are at an impasse.

Notwithstanding my having graciously invited John to clarify his position, the courteous approach has *not* opened his mind to further dialog. Even with an intended gracious delivery, this may be the unfortunate result. If hostility and self-justification lie in the heart, courtesy will likely be misunderstood and rebuffed.

It is human nature that no one wants to be challenged no matter how soft spoken and polite the words. The intellectual virtues alone cannot ensure a positive result. Courtesy and respectfulness may *not* open ears and lead to open-minded dialog.

It may well be, therefore, that the outraged anti-abortionist from the right and the fuming Trump hater on the left have both already thrown this book into their garbage bin. In light of Jesus's Sermon on the Mount, I called the anger of both unvirtuous. In spite of my attempt to set a tone of civility, I'm sure a few angry reactions may have set in. Sometimes it cannot be helped, and there is nothing more to be done.

With All Due Respect

It is common when about to introduce an opposing viewpoint, as I envisioned saying to John above, to use the phrase "with all due respect" without really meaning it. Hearing those words as a lead-in for "but I think you're wrong" gives the *due respect* a hollow ring and may set the defensiveness wheels of the brain beginning to turn.

However, an important truth lies in those words. Reminding ourselves of the point in the previous chapter, we are not called to respect an *idea* we consider wrong. We may not even respect the fact that an individual holds it. But we *are* called to respect that individual's humanity as a fellow child of God, equally created in his image. Jesus respected Peter as a man he loved, but he rebuked the idea Peter had allowed entry against the truth.

Perhaps another phrase would serve us better—a more lucid clarification of what is our real intent: "I'm sorry, but I disagree. At the same time, I honor and respect *you* because you are my brother or sister of the human family. I do not endorse the perspective you have voiced, but I value you as a man or woman, my neighbor of humanity."

I'm not suggesting we sprinkle our conversations with such sentiments. But something akin to this should be in our hearts as the undergirding basis for the courtesy and respect we want to demonstrate toward the *person*, even if not the idea. My wife, Judy, and I have made it a practice to devise words and phrases that convey our recognition of the individual–idea distinction in daily discourse. When helping our employees learn how to deal with disgruntled customers, we gave our people a list of soft and courteous words and phrases to use to deflect annoyance and prevent anger before it had a chance to gain a foothold. "Win them over with kindness" was the constant theme of our employee training.

This is equally important when dealing with contentious and potentially divisive ideas in the political realm. It is all the more vital for another reason: How will I respond when the shoe is on the other foot and *I* am the one challenged by a friend's exhortation?

If we hope to engage in honest, productive, fruitful dialog that keeps relationships respectful and growing, virtue has to flow in both directions. It is possible for kindness, honesty, humility, courtesy, and a listening spirit toward opposing perspectives to find common ground on which to meet similarly well-intentioned relational and intellectual virtues coming from the opposite side. We don't have to make enemies of those with opposite viewpoints.

And yet . . .

In the cultural cauldron of tumultuous change in which we find ourselves, there *is* bitterness, there *is* division, there *is* animosity, there *is* rudeness, there *is* judgment, there *is* rancor. It is in the air of the times. We cannot escape it.

May each of us pray, and mean it: *Let not these evils originate with me, nor find root in my heart.*

The Goal—Mutual Courtesy

What then is to be our response when the common ground of mutual courtesy does not exist?

The first question is whether or not courtesy is flowing from my lips. I need to make sure the problem isn't *me*. It is fearfully easy to delude ourselves at this point. No one wants to be told something they believe is wrong. While we may *think* we are behaving respectfully, another may not see it that way. The breakdown in civility and respect may be more my fault than I am willing to admit. It is hard, and takes ongoing and habitual effort, to assume the best—in nineteenth-century Scottish author's Henry Drummond's words, to put the best construction on the words and deeds of others whenever possible.[1] But hard or not, such is my half of the civility equation.

Moving beyond that, however, once I have honestly and humbly looked in the mirror, how ought I to carry myself when to the best of my ability I *am* attempting to demonstrate respect to an *individual* while disagreeing courteously with an *idea*, yet civility is met by rudeness and anger?

Where one side has no compunction to be civil, there's not much room for dialog. As in the case of John's angry response to the thoughtful question about his untruthfulness, civility is at an impasse. I can do nothing but quietly walk away, making sure John's anger does not become mutual.

This is the great challenge. Even kindness is often misread. Defensiveness is ever ready to impugn motive and hurl back false judgments. Civility will not ensure being treated respectfully in return. One can only influence one's own side of the relational equation. If civility is not mutual, it is best to lay down one's arms and walk away. Standing up for one's convictions will best be done at another time and in another way.

In such a circumstance, there will be real right and wrong involved. All responses are not created equal. It is wrong to return courtesy with rudeness. If John defensively throws courtesy back in my face and interprets my words as judgmental rather than as an honest attempt to speak on behalf of truth, he will be wrong to do so. He will have read into my words a reflection of his own anger. However, it won't be my job to tell him so. That would only throw gasoline on the fire of his anger.

The proper response, in an atmosphere of mutual respect, would be for John to say, "You are right. I was less than truthful. Thank you for holding that up to me. I need to go to the other people involved and ask forgiveness and make it right."

Mutual courtesy, humility, respect, intellectual honesty, reasonableness, and kindness *always* lead to good endings, relational wholeness, and an increase of truth.

But looking at the other side of the coin once again, it may be *me* who did not have all the facts. *I* may have been wrong in my assessment. Will I be mature enough, when the roles are reversed, to recognize it is *me* who has mis-reacted, and *I* am in the wrong?

If respect is operational in both directions, rather than taking offence, John might say, "I appreciate your coming to me. I know you have my best in mind, but let me tell you a little more about the situation and what was said."

Returning John's gracious and respectful response, now it is *my* turn to listen attentively, then reply, "Thank you for clarifying what happened. I see it more clearly. I appreciate your not taking offense at what I said. I'm sorry for misinterpreting the situation. Forgive me for drawing the wrong conclusion."

No anger. No hostility. Both John and I listened. We were each respectful of the other. I was shown where I had erred. Truth was advanced. And John and I took a step further toward relational maturity by handling a potentially contentious matter like men of truth.

20

COURAGE
the unvirtue: fear

Courage is not simply one of the virtues,
but the form of every virtue at the testing point.
— C. S. Lewis, *The Screwtape Letters*

Drawing heavily on the inspiration of Aleksandr Solzhenitsyn, as alluded to earlier, much of Rod Dreher's analysis of the current trends of our culture in his *Live Not by Lies* is based on the parallels he observes between the overt dictatorial totalitarianism of the former Soviet Union and the more obscure soft totalitarianism that is systematically undermining our freedoms at the hand of the progressivist agenda in twenty-first-century America. We are not being thrown into prison by the KGB for opposing the totalitarianism of an all-powerful communist police state. But those who do not give allegiance to the new, enlightened, liberal America *are* increasingly marginalized, ostracized, and silenced—a gentler form of societal prison more in keeping with *soft* totalitarianism. Dreher is translating Francis Schaeffer's warnings, from what now seems another era altogether, into the reality of our own time.* Schaeffer's warnings from almost fifty years ago are summarized in appendix 2.

---

* The very titles of some of Schaeffer's books tell the tale even if one hasn't read them: *Escape from Reason*, *The Church Before the Watching World*, *The Great Evangelical Disaster*, *Whatever Happened to the Human Race?*, *How Should We Then Live?: The Rise and Decline of Western Thought and Culture*, and his final book, *A Christian Manifesto*.

The Cultural Thought Police

The new liberal elite Schaeffer foresaw needs no army. Neither does it need a Gestapo or KGB. Its indoctrinated citizenry has made of itself a Cultural Thought Police (CTP) force.* Its unwritten marching orders are to detect and root out then persuade and browbeat dissenters who have not yet fallen in with the ideals of the new progressive order.

As the KGB enforced the mandated perspectives of the Politburo, it is the moral duty (as they see it) of the civilian CTP to make certain those in their spheres—workplace, school, church, social gatherings, extended families—embrace the new ideas laid down by the Agenda, vote accordingly, and speak no word of opposition. Those who do not go along will be branded as backward, ignorant, racist, unenlightened, judgmental, and hateful. How interesting that, along with such classics as *To Kill a Mockingbird* and *Of Mice and Men*, George Orwell's two prophetic classics that expose the lies of progressivism so perceptively—*1984* and *Animal Farm*—are also now banned from many U.S. school libraries.†

Condescension is usually the CTP's first retaliatory technique. Conservative thinkers not in step with the times will initially be laughed at as fools. If they are passive and can be humiliated into silence, that may be enough. But if they vocally express themselves and persist in their opposition, reprisals become increasingly severe. Eventually they will be punished, shunned, lied about, excommunicated, and, if possible, professionally destroyed. These reprisals will

---

* My term. Others have used the term Social Justice Warriors (SJW) for this new civilian, Gestapo-like network of eyes watching their friends, relatives, and neighbors for violations of the agenda.

† These four along with *Fahrenheit 451* and *Lord of the Flies* are among Barnes and Noble's top-ten banned book list. Examples of such things are too numerous to mention. The following is from *Newsweek*'s January 24, 2023, online issue: "Schools in Burbank will no longer be able to teach a handful of classic novels, including Harper Lee's *To Kill a Mockingbird,* following concerns raised by parents over racism . . . . Until further notice, teachers in the area will not be able to include on their curriculum Harper Lee's *To Kill a Mockingbird,* Mark Twain's *The Adventures of Huckleberry Finn,* John Steinbeck's *Of Mice and Men,* Theodore Taylor's *The Cay,* and Mildred D. Taylor's *Roll of Thunder, Hear My Cry.* Four parents, three of whom are Black, challenged the classic novels for alleged potential harm to the district's roughly 400 Black students."

undoubtedly get worse. Imprisonments have already begun for no actual *crime* as the term has been traditionally understood but for the "idea-crime" of refusing to comply with certain progressive mandates that violate one's conscience.

The progression of retribution against dissent varies but proceeds from less to more forceful methods. Initial ridicule and condescension eventually give way to full-blown loathing against the most determined and powerful dissidents against the Agenda. Whomever they hate, the CTP must destroy. This they accomplish with many tactics to undermine credibility, thus insuring that potentially influential opponents cannot ultimately harm the righteous cause of progressivism.

In its "kinder and gentler tactics," the CTP can be as ruthless as the KGB, while carrying out its idea-pogrom with the smiling air of self-righteousness.

A National Lightning Rod

Donald Trump represents the prototypical example how the process works. Bringing him into the discussion because he is a lightning rod of diverse and heated reaction on both Left and Right is potentially divisive. But because he has loomed large on the national stage in recent years and continues to influence the nation's political narrative—whether one loves him or hates him or laughs at him—his example is instructive. It illuminates how the Left responds when vigorously challenged. Even Trump's most vociferous opponents and detractors will do well to learn from both his successes and his failures. His example reveals much about the cultural war in which all who love truth are engaged—both what to do and what not to do.

When Donald Trump announced for the presidency, the Left laughed and dismissed him as a buffoon. If laughter is the best medicine, it is also the Left's first best weapon. Nothing stings quite like ridicule.*

---

* Another of Saul Alinsky's Rules for Radicals, #5: "Ridicule is man's most potent weapon. . . ." It is little wonder that Hillary Clinton, whose senior thesis at Wellesley was devoted to the teachings of Saul Alinsky, so often replied to hard questions with laughter. She was attempting to dismiss the import of the questions with ridicule.

But Trump fought back. Even after winning the Republican nomination, however, and throughout the 2016 campaign, his opposition couldn't bring itself to take a man they viewed as a blowhard seriously. The entire country knew he couldn't win. On the day of the election, the liberal media had still not progressed beyond the level of condescension.

Twenty-four hours later, the CTP was no longer laughing. Its righteous indignation immediately shifted into high gear, devising means to punish, marginalize, and shun both him and his "deplorable" followers. Long before he was even inaugurated as president, impeachment plans were underway. Any pretense of a justification would do—constitutional or not.

Contingency plans also began to ensure, if he survived impeachment, that he would *never* be reelected. The Russian collusion investigation was the *piece de resistance,* a fabricated conspiracy founded on invention and innuendo in which the highest levels of government and the opposition campaign were complicit. It was as close to a coup to oust a sitting president as the United States has ever seen—Congress and the justice department essentially colluding against the executive branch of the government.

For four years the attacks were unrelenting—as they always will be against those who publicly resist the Agenda. Failing to remove him from office during his tenure, the slow methodical accusations ultimately succeeded in ousting him from power. By then, however, getting him out of Washington was not enough. Hatred had taken over, and it was far from satiated. Hatred is indeed a powerful intoxicant. His opponents finally succeeded in excommunicating him from social media. He was cut off, emasculated, and all the while legal charges against him continued. Even then, however, he was still not destroyed.

This is no attempt to paint Trump as a martyr or victim-hero of the embattled Right. He is a "type," the reaction to whom illustrates the same protocol used against thousands, even millions whose names will never be known who have dared raise their voices against the Agenda. These millions, out of the public spotlight, whose stories will never be told, have been victimized by the same tactics on a smaller scale as were played out on the national stage by the drama of Donald Trump vs. progressivism.

Humiliation, ridicule, anger, criticism, condescension, and false accusation gradually increase in intensity until shunning, excommunication, and professional ruin are all leveled against the most recalcitrant. This and far more will be employed openly as the ideological war intensifies. Those who stand for traditional American values and the truths of Christianity will not merely be viewed as misguided opponents; they will be *hated*.

A New KGB Is in Our Midst

Freedom to think for oneself is being eradicated from the national scene. It has already been virtually eliminated from college and university campuses. Free speech, freedom of the press (book banning), and freedom of dissent (social media censorship) are already on the chopping block. Freedom of religion, so called, is next. In reality, only Christianity is under attack. Islam in America has never enjoyed more freedom.

By 2020, the new soft totalitarianism had taken over large segments of American life, society, and politics. Academia, the media, and Hollywood illustrate but the most obvious examples. The most chilling reality is that the Cultural Thought Police wear no uniforms, carry no guns. Its invisible legions are all around us—our friends, neighbors, family members, church acquaintances, workplace colleagues. They do not report your violations of the progressive code to Moscow. They mete out your punishment themselves. It is *they* who ostracize and marginalize you, who spread the quiet word that you are different, not one of them, not in step with the new ways of thinking. You need to be squeezed out, kept from influence, made of no effect. You are a pariah, an enemy of the commonweal.*

---

* They may also sue you. A number of recent lawsuits have been filed, mostly in educational environments, on the basis of pronoun use.

The louder your voice of dissent, the more energetic the Trump Protocol will be brought against you. Elon Musk, long the darling of entrepreneurial prowess, came under attack as a racist employer. His crime against liberalism was the suggestion that free speech ought to apply to conservatives too—and this was his unforgivable sin—even to Donald Trump. Racism is always one of the first weapons employed against opponents of the Agenda. It doesn't matter if the charge is completely imaginary. The poison dart of racism, false though it may be, can be professionally fatal.

With his usual wry wit, C. S. Lewis anticipated the CTP when he wrote, "Of all tyrannies, a tyranny sincerely exercised for the good of its victims may be the most oppressive. It would be better to live under robber barons than under omnipotent moral busybodies. The robber baron's cruelty may sometimes sleep, his cupidity may at some point be satiated; but those who torment us for our own good will torment us without end for they do so with the approval of their own conscience."[1]

It is not a kinder, gentler KGB. The CTP may be subtle, but it is anything but kind. It is cruel, deceitful, single-minded, and ruthless. To survive in good standing, you must ignore Solzhenitsyn's warning. You *must* live by the lies.

If you choose to oppose the lies, to speak against them, you will pay the price.

The Trump Protocol

Groupspeak explains the presidential election of 2016 and why the pundits and pollsters got it wrong. The narrative hammered home 24/7 by the news media was that Donald Trump was a buffoon and fool, and so was anyone who supported him—phase 1 of the Trump Protocol. Groupspeak became a powerful force throughout the country. Trump supporters learned to keep their mouths shut. Democrats assumed they had the election in the bag. It was the "perceived consensus" of a perceived majority.

When election day came, however, in the privacy of the voting booth, groupspeak hadn't been altogether numbing to individuality. Shielded from the eyes of the CTP, men and women who *could* think for themselves elected Donald Trump president. The next day the more sinister methods of the Trump Protocol were set in motion.

The rest is already fading into the rearview mirror of presidential history. The conspiracy against him achieved its purpose. After a brief four-year hiatus, the Lie was back in power. The Agenda had been preserved. Progressivism could continue its march toward its appointed destiny even more rapidly, and more deviously and untruthfully, than before.

Courage Must Be Augmented with Humility and Authenticity

Some may recoil at using Donald Trump as an example of courage. Trump hatred continues to blind as many eyes to objective truth as did Obama worship. But who can deny that the former president possessed courage to call out the Lie, to dare say that the progressive emperor was wearing no clothes?

But while he exemplified a key virtue, Mr. Trump's example also stands as an important warning to those who would heed Aleksandr Solzhenitsyn's challenge. His courage was not given stature by the corresponding integrity of personal character that could have made him a historically significant leader. The example—virtuous though it might be—had a dark opposite side that ultimately led to his downfall—his *political* downfall. His *personal* fortunes and future and the eternal story being written on his heart, only God sees into whatever those developments may be.

Donald Trump's fatal flaw (speaking politically) was a flaw of personal character. He could not find within himself the humility to lay aside his natural bombastic, derisive, self-aggrandizing ego. The universal battle between flesh and spirit, between our inner demons and the better angels of our nature, was sadly a battle that he was ill-equipped to wage as he stood on the national stage.

That he was, in one sense, an "authentic" man, cannot be denied. If anything, Donald Trump was authentically *himself.* He was who he was and was proud of it. When attacked, he fought back with vengeance. When asked why he did not adopt a calmer, more conciliatory, gentler, less arrogant and braggadocios style—that of a courteous and respectful statesman—those closest to him always gave the same answer, "You can't stop him from being himself. He is who he is."

While one must respect a man, as desperately as he wanted to win, willing to run the risk of losing an election rather than being untrue to himself—which cannot be said of many politicians—Mr. Trump's insistence on "being himself" also represents the ultimate political foolishness. After four years in the Oval Office, if he had met the unrelenting attacks against him with statesmanlike stature of character and graciousness of demeanor, he would surely have been reelected in 2020. That he could not raise his personal character to the stature worthy of the office, therefore, also demonstrates an intrinsic character flaw that undermined the very courage he brought to the battle against progressivism. Humility, graciousness, kindness, and love for his kind (including those who hated him), when combined with his natural courage and the force of his personality, might truly have been significant to shift the course of the nation toward truth, or at least slowed the drift. As it was, however, he proved an ineffective standard-bearer in the ideological war.

The Virtues Work in Harmony

Donald Trump did not allow himself to grow into depth of character and personal maturity to reflect fully authentic integrity of personhood. Virtue had not sent roots deep enough into his being. The authenticity of Christlikeness was not a visible component of his character. Whether or not it was the subject of his prayers and the objective of his inner life, I am not privy to those eternal workings.

All the virtues work in harmony. While Donald Trump was fearless, guileless, and bold, too many unvirtues were endemic to his public persona. His example is vital to everyone who may feel called to speak their convictions, even if only around the Thanksgiving dinner table. Words mean little—even words that may be true and boldly and courageously spoken—if they are not accompanied by authenticity of Christlikeness and a character of humility, kindness, gentleness, graciousness, and love. Our former president exemplifies why *virtue* is the subject of this book and the only weapon that will win the ideological war.

To echo a similar progression from the apostle Paul, let courage be empowered by humility, boldness invigorated by quiet fearlessness, honesty animated by personal dignity, and above all may we put on love.

Courage to speak may not be the most important kind of courage. Internal courage to be God's authentic sons and daughters, reflecting *him* not our pride, reflecting *his* character not our own willfulness, reflecting the quiet courage of Jesus when facing the great Lie, is the courage that will defeat the Lie.

How many does it take to change a culture? It takes one with courage.

And thus we come to one of the most important virtues of all.

21

INTEGRITY
the unvirtue: fragmentation

The life of a good religious person ought to be adorned with all virtues;
that he may inwardly be such as outwardly he seems to men.
— Thomas à Kempis

Many words might be used to encapsulate the full scope of what comprises "virtue." One of the most powerful is the familiar word *integrity*. A familiar word, yes. Not so well understood. Still less fully *lived* in the trenches of life.

Oneness

Dictionary definitions are not always the best place to begin, but they can bring useful clarity to concepts that have become particularly ambiguous in this era of "useless words." *Integrity* has suffered from exactly that ambiguity. It rouses many diverse ideas in our minds, yet its meaning is straightforward and clear. Think of the word *integer*. It is the mathematical term for a single whole number. The first and primary integer is the number 1.

That's integrity—*wholeness, oneness.*

In its simplest terms, integrity means *strong*, *whole*, and *sound*—the *integer* of character. In other words, containing no blemishes or imperfections, a perfect "one." In the mathematical world—no fractions, no fragments, nothing left over. A piece of wood with a crack is *not* sound. It will split under pressure. It has no "structural integrity." Improperly mixed concrete or improperly tempered steel do not give integrity to the foundation of a building. Both are structurally weak. The integrity of the building is compromised.

This basic meaning of integrity indicating underlying, often invisible, makeup and strength is a condition of physicality. But when transferred to the world of morals and personal character, integrity takes on its most powerful import. In that context it rises to express the composite structural *oneness* of all the virtues—soundness of character, without cracks or splits, fragments or weaknesses that would undermine the integral fabric and strength and moral fiber of the complete individual.

From Webster's Dictionary: "Wholeness, entireness . . . . [T]he . . . unimpaired state of any thing, particularly of the mind; moral soundness . . . honesty. . . . [T]he whole moral character but has special reference to uprightness. . . . Purity; genuine, unadulterated."[1]

A Committee of Divergent Selves

The spiritual implications are enormous and yet not always obvious. Our inner selves are more split, unwhole, and fragmented than we care to admit. We are not *whole* numbers. We are *fractional* numbers and not just because we are weak, growing, and imperfect human beings though that is an obvious part of it. More worrisome, however, or it *ought* to be more worrisome, is that we intentionally choose this fragmentation over the complete unity and soundness of our whole selves. We *choose* to fragment and compartmentalize our spiritual selves into a fractional collection of different selves who live inconsistently with one another. *We* create the cracks in the grains of our characters, the imperfections in the concrete of our foundations. Then we accommodate ourselves to them, hardly realizing to what an extent they weaken the structural fabric of who we are.

Thomas Kelly pinpointed it exactly. "The outer distractions of our interests," he wrote, "reflect an inner lack of integration of our own lives. We are trying to be several selves at once, without all our selves being organized by a single, mastering Life within us. Each of us tends to be, not a single self, but a whole committee of selves."[2]

These distinct "selves" are not only inconsistent; they are often in direct conflict. They create fissures and weaknesses in the character-foundation. We live with them because we have chosen them. We become so accustomed to the inconsistencies we hardly notice.

- I am a Christian. I realize I am commanded to love and forgive those who wrong me. But I am not about to forgive him, not after what he did!

That statement reveals a spiritual crack at the core of personhood. Where is the integrity, the wholeness of purpose, motive, and choice—the unity and oneness of personhood?

- I am commanded as a Christian to live in purity, not so much as to allow the hint or appearance of evil into my demeanor. However, I choose to wear low-cut blouses knowing full well that men will "look."
- I am commanded to lifelong fidelity, but I choose to file for divorce.
- We're both Christians, but we've decided to move in together before getting married.
- I believe in being a good witness, but I don't worry too much about my language. I don't want people thinking of me as a goody two shoes.

All these reveal gaping fissures at the virtue-foundations of spiritual personhood—a lack of virtue-diligence in the corners. How can Christians influence the world for virtue when they're not living the virtue-commands of the Bible any more visibly than the people of the world. It's a variation of the RINO acronym (Republicans in name only). Such inconsistencies, and thousands of others, reveal the Christians-in-name-only integrity problem plaguing Christendom.

Such fragmentations and inconsistencies between our inner "committee of selves" abound. That there are no blatantly immoral fragmentations in my life does not excuse me from examining my *own* integrity quotient in the mirror. I violate the integrity of wholeness in my own ways, too, allowing my choices to split my inner self into competing selves trying to take me in opposing directions.

The forces pulling us apart, fragmenting our motives and choices, are daily and persistent. We make the choice whether to be men and women of integrity a dozen times a day. Integrity never emerges from drift, from placing the will on autopilot. Integrity requires alertness, the courage of hard choices, alertness to the signs of the times, refusing to heed the voices from the various committee chairmen shouting for attention.

Integrity—wholeness of purpose, singleness of eye, constancy of motive—is a hard-won virtue. It is a virtue of strength, valor, and courage that is won in the trenches where decisions and choices are made. Those daily choices move us, one step at a time, toward wholeness of direction, motive, and purpose—or toward fragmentation.

National Centers of Fragmentation That Breed Character Drift

It is difficult to imagine a more transparently fragmented and cowardly body of men and women than those who gather in the halls of Congress, the White House, and in the capitals of the fifty states. There are isolated exceptions to be sure. But even what is usually lauded as *courage* in those centers of power is little more than boldness and bravado in standing for one's party platform. And every two years the populace brings yet more fragmented men and women, void of the integrity of personhood, into the national spotlight where character virtue is despised and outspoken unreason and illogic are lauded.

I have said this is not *primarily* a political book. Yet something is wrong with us as a people that we allow such fragmentation between special interests, party affiliation, and political correctness to represent us. It is no secret we are a fragmented nation, torn in opposite directions. Such a dearth of *integrity* exists at the top of the nation's leadership that our country has lost its moral compass. Why do we allow the direction of our nation to be guided by a moral bankruptcy that has abandoned its sense of right and wrong? Why do concerned Americans and Christians continue to elect men and women who do not possess the inner integrity to stand as whole, complete, integritous people devoted to truth? This is a great mystery that strikes at the heart of a national conscience that seems to have gone into a coma.

At the time of this writing, what are possibly the two most egregious examples of the absurd and horrifying lack of integrity in Washington and the statehouses are surely transgender athletics and postbirth abortion—the *absurdity* of pretending that young men are girls and the *horrifying* murder, which seems to be on the way, of *living* human babies. Many other examples exist, but these are so unbelievable one wonders how otherwise intelligent men and women can have so completely forsaken reason as to think them normal and acceptable.

Everyone knows that both cross the line of ethics, reason, goodness, and righteousness. *Everyone* knows they are wrong. In their heart of hearts, all one hundred senators and 435 congressmen and -women know that they cross the line of right and wrong. The women who allow their babies to be killed know it is wrong. The transgender athletes pretending to be what they're not know it's wrong.

But none will admit it. Instead of recognizing the obvious, they go along with the pretext. They are too weak of character to stand in the integrity of wholeness. So they allow the fragmentation between right and wrong to turn them into political eunuchs and mute cowards. To say, "I value life," and yet support abortion is fragmentation. The two halves of such a nature are pointed in opposite directions. To say, "I believe in justice for all," and support transgender athletics is fragmentation. The man or woman standing in the divide between those opposites cannot be said to reflect integrity in his or her personal life.

The rest of us are fragmented, too, electing men and women who are so blind to the imperative of integrity that with straight faces they cast votes approving these atrocities. They ought to be either laughing or crying when they cast their yea votes for such preposterous absurdities. That they do so with passionless expressions is all the evidence needed that integrity has left the building.

Who are we to complain? We put these mute ethical eunuchs in power. Do we care about our nation's moral fiber so little?

Where have all the flowers gone? Where has wholeness gone? What has become of true leadership?

We are called to integrity, to be whole men and women, for all the constituent parts of our personality and character to be integrated into a unity of personhood. This does not make us perfect. But in the midst of our flaws, we are intended to be whole, of a single piece. Our lives will never be entirely whole, but our motives can be perfect. Unity of motive, the *desire* for the complex aspects of our nature to be moving in the same direction, toward the same goal, is one of the most fundamental ingredients that make up integrity.

How many does it take to change a culture? It takes one with integrity.

Our weapon is virtue, lived with integrity.

22

AUTHORITY
the unvirtue: independence

*Christianity became the official state religion early in the fourth century,
and with this new status began an unfortunate secularization of the Church.
When the Christian faith was mixed with the Roman world,
the world did not become Christian so much as Christians became worldly.*

— Richard Foster and James Bryan Smith, *Devotional Classics*

Authority and submission are among the most hated concepts of our time. Yet authority is *the* foundational principle of the universe. The entire creation was formed by authority. It is by authority that it is sustained. Authority is embedded into every atom of the universe.

Therefore, without a healthy and abiding, not mere recognition of authority but *love* of authority and its primal place in the world at the root of all things, virtue will not have the right soil in which to grow, flourish, and bear fruit.

Authority—The Undergirding Fabric of a Nation

The *absolute Authority* in the universe, of course, is God, its creator and the sustainer of its life. This is a far more important statement than a mere matter of religious belief. It is clear in our own time that not everyone believes in God at all. However, we are seeking truth about our country and its future. Authority—anchored in belief in God's authority as the one *Absolute* in life—is the solid foundation upon which everything in the structure and fabric of our nation is built. Our laws, our awareness of right and wrong, societal order, the Constitution (the country's structure of Authority), the Supreme Court (our supreme legal Authority) are all rooted in authority. We could also include such agencies as the IRS, the FBI, the EPA—*everything* functions on the basis of authority. Without Authority, there could be no nationhood, no United States of America.

All men and women recognize the existence and need for authority. Yet most hate authority when its reality intrudes into their personal lives. They don't mind being the one *in* authority. They hate being *answerable* to authority.

Why is the idea of authority so hated? It is another example of fragmentation—of wanting to go in two directions at once. We want to retain the order and structure of society and nationhood (the Constitution, the legal system, the Supreme Court, and our many national institutions), but we do not want to *personally* submit to that authority when we don't feel like it. Personal independence is the god of our age.* As long as authority keeps its hands off my independence, I won't complain. But let it get too close, watch out!

We are thus a schizophrenic people, torn in multiple directions. We have laws (authority), yet radical progressives want to defund the police because they don't like the police *enforcing* the laws. We claim to be a nation of law, yet progressives want to ignore immigration laws and voting laws they perceive as inconvenient to the Agenda. We say that we are a nation that reveres justice (authority), but we turn a blind eye to the injustice of transgender athletics, reverse-racism, and discrimination against Christian businesses and organizations. So-called social justice is one of the new idols of progressivism, which is likewise founded in *injustice* and discrimination toward certain groups.

---

* I refer here to *personal* independence—no one will tell *me* what to do! The idol of personal independence, of course, along with those equally worshipped idols of equity and rights, spread their cancers out into the culture in myriad ways. These must be distinguished from their good and noble and virtuous counterparts. Our Declaration of Independence and Constitution and Bill of Rights are all founded on the noble ideal of human *equality*, of the *right* to be free and *independent*. It is unfortunate that the same word is used for two altogether different qualities.

Fragmentation abounds. This schizophrenic application of the principle of authority sits at the bull's eye in the ideological war along with the modern idol of independence. This represents more than a debate about the existence of God but one which strikes at the core of the fundamental order of a society and culture and its myriad interconnected hierarchies of authority.* Does law apply in the same way to the illegal immigrant and the white Christian businessman whose convictions will not allow him to hire a gay or lesbian? Does the illegal foreigner get a free pass, while the Christian's business is shut down and its owner sued? Does independence to do whatever one likes apply to BLM and Antifa but not to Christians?

How we respond to authority as a nation is at the crux of our national debate. Thus it may be appropriate to reflect briefly on the origin of this all-important component of virtue upon which our nation was built.

Authority in Genesis

Contrary to prevailing modern thinking, the answers to many, probably most, of life's quandaries are rooted in the first three chapters of the Bible. The practical life-meaning of these chapters is the same

---

* Hierarchies of descending authority are obvious in any business organizational chart (from CEO to office clerk), in government (from federal to state to local), and in the personal/spiritual realm (from God to his ordained spokesmen—Jesus at the top, of course, and apostles, prophets, pastors, etc.—to ancestral family structure to fathers and mothers to children). All these God-ordained hierarchies are fragmenting in our culture from the underlying repudiation of authority as a founding and necessary principle of life and the world. In our day, too, the pseudo-virtue of equality, morphing now into equity, has permeated all segments of society. Every group and individual needs to be considered "equal" to everyone else in every way (citizens equal to noncitizens, criminals equal to police, tenants equal to landlords, those with less money equal to and deserving of the same income as those with more money). Those in authority, especially *men* at the top of hierarchy structures (more so if they are *white* men), are targets of unrelenting criticism, blame, and constant scrutiny. Of course there are abuses of authority. No one denies they should be corrected. But progressivism's attempt to equalize every aspect of life has not only contributed to the erosion of authority but also to a completely unrealistic and unsustainable model for how life and relationships, businesses and families and nations actually function.

no matter how old one believes the earth is, or whether one believes Adam and Eve were a literal man and woman or are mythological characters. What matters is that the universe was created by God out of nothing. It was created by the power and intrinsic beingness of infinite Authority.

This is the foundational essence, the *meaning*, of the opening verse of the Bible: *God created.*

Sheer Authority.

Let there be . . . and there was.

Let there be a firmament . . . and it was so.

Let the waters be gathered . . . and it was so.

Let the earth . . . and it was so.

Let there be light . . . and it was so.

Let the earth bring forth . . . and it was so.

Then God said, "Let us make man . . . ."

And God saw that it was good.

The first, primary, essential, imperative foundation stone everything in life is built upon is the resounding Truth revealed in every line of Genesis 1–3: *Authority.* The futile yearning for autonomous independence, the utopian fancy that we are free and self-ruling agents answerable to no one, is a poison fruit of modernism.

The foundation of life's meaning begins with the acknowledgment of God's supreme and ultimate authority. His authority extends over all creation, over the universe, over every living thing, over every man and woman and child, over you and me.

Truth begins, meaning begins, wisdom begins, personhood begins, virtue begins in the acknowledgment of God's authority.

What, then, does authority imply? It implies *command*. Authority expresses its will by command, not suggestion, debate, discussion, or persuasion.

Authority is the noun; command is the verb by which authority acts.

God *commanded* creation. "Let there be!" is the ultimate statement of command. And the command of authority was obeyed: *There was light.*

The very fact of authority necessitates the essential imperative of command as the mechanism by which authority delivers its ruling will. Authority does not attempt to talk its subjects into doing its will. It *commands* obedience to its will.

Yet *command* is also a noun. A fact. By the authoritative fact of command, God commanded the universe and all matter in it, the heavens and its galaxies and stars and planets and moons, the earth and its waters and inanimate growing things, its laws, its motions, its science, its changes and growth and expansion and evolutionary development.

And all the universe *obeyed*.

America's Foundation Is Rooted in the Authority of Genesis

This is no mere religious homily on Genesis. These resounding truths—authority, command, obedience—are the foundation stones our nation's founders built upon. Our laws and Constitution—the authority and "God" of the nation, so to speak—command certain things. Those commands are to be obeyed. It's how the country works.

Our nation is founded on authority, command, and obedience.

That's why the first three chapters of Genesis matter. This is no mere detour of interest only to religious readers. The roots of the United States of America extend straight back into the soil of Genesis 1–3.

According to progressivism, however, certain of those laws and undergirding principles can now be changed to suit the authority-hatred of changing times. We'll disregard the law and the Constitution so that we can legalize the travesty of abortion or same-sex marriage, not to mention theft and adultery and destruction of property and immigration laws and whatever other standards and legalities and virtues we find inconvenient. We'll justify them by pretending that such is what the Constitution really *ought* to mean—that such is actually what the founders would have wanted all along, had they been able to see into the future. We'll change the laws to legalize anything we want. Better yet, we'll ignore the law and Constitution altogether—just like we ignore God and *his* authority and *his* commands.

The Death of Authority

The state of the political divide in our nation can be explained in its simplest terms by the death of authority as our founding principle of nationhood. It is little wonder that authority is so little valued as a virtue among liberals. The roots of today's liberalism extend back to the 1960s, to the anti-establishment movement when one of the most popular bumper stickers plastered on VW buses read "Resist Authority." That slogan remains the mantra of progressivism.

Today's liberals are the scions of 1960s radicals. Hillary Clinton might be seen as leading the vanguard of this sixties radicalism coming of age, with her husband, Bill, and the Obamas following in her wake. Hillary learned her tactics under militant activist Saul Alinsky, whose *Rules for Radicals* is still the manual for the Left.

A new generation has now risen up under wannabe future president, current New York congresswoman Alexandria Ocasio-Cortez (AOC), whose tactics will eventually make the Clintons and Obamas seem like Republicans. The progressive tolerance of BLM and Antifa reveals that at the heart of liberalism, violent, lawless sixties radicalism still reigns. By the time she may rise to the summit, AOC or her protégé will likely have many such "squads" throughout the country enforcing her agenda.

Whatever side one happens to be on in the political divide, any objective observer can see that authority as an undergirding virtue is more respected by conservatives than by liberals. Respect for law is virtually dead within liberalism. In general terms, conservatives have not given up on America's founding principles. Respect of law still means something at the heart of conservatism.

This explains why Bob Dole and Mitt Romney were gracious in defeat. The Republican rank and file did not go after Obama with foolish impeachment charges after 2008. They may not have considered him a wise or virtuous man, but they respected authority. Except for a few vocal outliers, most Republicans accepted the election results without taking to the streets with violence.

Hillary, on the other hand, betrayed her hatred of authority after 2016 by continually questioning the legitimacy of the election so as to pave the way for the move for impeachment. Following her lead, the Democrat machine set about to devise some means to oust the new president. If progressives don't like a law, they ignore it. If they don't like an election, they try to overturn it. For four years liberals tried to impeach and convict President Trump then bring legal charges against him to keep him from running again. Its hatred was completely out of bounds for one reason: liberals do not respect authority unless it is in their hands, where they can manipulate it to their own ends.

Donald Trump behaved no better four years later—the unvirtues are no respecter of party lines. But he cannot be viewed as typical of the Republican party in general. His contesting of the election was but following Hillary's playbook.

This difference between conservative and progressive respect for authority has been glaringly apparent in the national discourse for several election cycles. Of course this is a broad generalization. Different views are hotly debated. But conservatives, in general (not all but in general), hold to a faintly gentlemanly sense of decorum that was once also evident among the classic liberals of former generations. Sadly it is nearly completely invisible on the new progressive liberal Left. Conservatives have their bombastic blow-hards too. No one will deny that. But authority remains a valued commodity in spite of them.

Seeds Must Be Planted One at a Time

All this being true, however, gets us no nearer to the practicalities of virtue that we hope will make a difference in the ideological war. Arguing about the Left's abandonment of authority will accomplish little if we are not willing to put our money where our mouths are and live by authority ourselves. The virtues must be lived if they are to have power and influence, even if your example or mine only plants a seed in one heart. That heart may be an impressionable youngster or teen who, thirty years from now, may be a U.S. senator whose life perspective was given a nudge toward truth by observing *you* stand respectfully, quietly, and confidently for truth in the corner of the world where you live. You never knew it, but the seed of your example went into the soil of his character and sprouted.

Well-planted seeds grow.

Let us, therefore, not just read Genesis 1–3 as an ancient text to debate but as a picture of how the universe works. May you and I live this day in the reality of "Let there be"—in the reality of authority, command, and obedience as founding principles of the world and of our nation.

That future senator may be watching.

23

PURITY
the unvirtue: impurity

Humility is the safeguard of chastity. In the matter of purity,
there is no greater danger than not fearing the danger.
— Philip Neri

Along with authority, purity may be the most neglected virtue of our time.

We have emphasized the importance of many virtues—we could consider dozens! We've included in this discussion only those that impact the national virtue of our country and, seen in this light, are in grave danger. Purity sits near the top of that endangered list.

Sad to say, Christians have contributed as much as the secular world for putting it there. Purity disappeared from the world a long time ago. But the church has gone along with the world's loose morals to such an extent that purity, chastity, modesty, and decorum have now all but vanished from the landscape of Christendom. The word *chastity* is not even listed in Microsoft's thesaurus. Society wants to normalize sexual depravity and strike chastity from the dictionary.

Sexual Impurity—The Worst Form of Unvirtue

Impurity, of course, takes many forms. We are all impure of thought in diverse ways, not all of them sexual. Avarice wears diverse faces—lust for food, possessions, money, power. These are all impure in their own way—violations of right and truth, wholeness and integrity. Yet realistically, who hasn't thought, *It would be nice to have more money.* It's natural.

That's not to excuse it. Gratitude and contentment are high personal virtues. But we are able to put such thoughts into perspective with the virtue of common sense. The impact on character is not of huge severity unless we *act* on our desire for more money and rob a bank.

It is *sexual* purity that is on the endangered-virtues list—*moral* purity and *marital* fidelity. Rampant sexual promiscuity is sending our nation down a bottomless pit of hedonism, wantonness, and self-indulgence.

A major distinction exists between sexual impurity and impure thoughts. Sexual impurity is *enormously* destructive to character. We recognize that Jesus equated lust with committing adultery in the heart. But lust is not the same as acting on it. There comes a time to turn away and *not* rob the bank.

Sexual purity is a *choice*. No one transgresses sexually by accident. *Every* sexual violation is willful and chosen. No one accidentally has an affair. "It just happened" is one of the stupidest justifications for sexual transgression imaginable. There is *always* a moment to turn away from a compromising situation. "It just happened" is another way of saying, "I chose *not* to turn away. I willfully *chose* to sin."

Sex never "just happens."*

It is the choice to sin that leaves such an unhealable scar across character. All sin can be forgiven. But sexual sin can never be entirely *healed*. Once done, it's *done*.

God takes sexual purity so seriously that almost every potential act of impure sexual activity is specifically mentioned in Leviticus 18. God *hates* sexual impurity. He uses the strongest possible language to characterize sexual sin—disobedience, perversion, defilement, and wickedness. Those are powerful words of condemnation for what our culture considers perfectly acceptable. A number of the violations listed were punishable by death. Among these was the practice of

---

* The command is from 1 Timothy 5:22. Obviously, however, there are exceptions. Rape and abuse clearly change this dynamic. Those are severe issues no one takes lightly. They are serious societal scourges, and we all recognize them as such.

homosexuality. God hates sexual perversion of *all* kinds. A modernist may scoff, but God takes sexuality *very* seriously.

Being acted on by chosen premeditated *choice*, purity is unique among the virtues in a very important way. It is possible to be *perfectly* virtuous—to be 100 percent sexually pure over an entire lifetime. This can be said about few virtues. The biblical injunction, "Be pure" is one that can be obeyed perfectly.

Purity Is Not to Be Taken Lightly

The following are violations of purity because they represent willful choices to *act* on the temptation, the lust, the desire, the urge, the impulse—to rob the bank rather than recognizing the wrong and turn from it.

- Premarital sex is a chosen and willful violation of purity.
- Adultery is a chosen and willful violation of purity.
- Living a homosexual lifestyle is a chosen and willful violation of purity.
- Lying is a chosen and willful violation of purity.
- Same-sex marriage is a chosen and willful violation of purity.
- Transgenderism is a chosen and willful violation of purity.
- Profanity is a chosen and willful violation of purity.
- Immodest or provocative dress in both women and men are chosen and willful violations of purity.
- Flirting is a chosen and willful violation of purity.
- All forms of pornography are chosen and willful violations of purity.
- Crude jokes are chosen and willful violations of purity.
- Pretending to tolerate and laugh at lewd comments is a chosen and willful violation of purity.
- Condoning the impurity of others is a chosen and willful violation of purity.
- Teasing or snubbing those who chose a life of purity is a chosen and willful violation of purity.

All these are on full display among Christians before a watching world. If you know what you are looking for, half of them may secretly exist in the pews in most churches on any given Sunday morning. Is it any wonder the world has not been won to Christ and is in a virtue-crisis when Christians care so little about obeying the straightforward biblical command, "Be pure."

It's not a "Do the best you can," command.

It's a 100 percent command:

> Be *perfectly* pure sexually
> > *after* marriage
> > > toward one, and *only* one
> > > > *lifetime* marital mate
> > > > > of the *opposite* sex.

God's command is unambiguous.

If you are not committed to visible purity in morals and ethics, dress and behavior, you will pass on seeds of unvirtue not virtue. This is where the virtue-crisis begins and ends. When you women look in your closet and see only low-cut sweaters and blouses and dresses, do you have the virtue hunger to get rid of them and invest in a new wardrobe that conveys discretion, modesty, and purity? Do you have the courage as a Christian woman to walk in modesty rather than trying to call attention to what no Christian woman should want men looking at? When you men choose movies and television programs to watch, do you change the channel or get up and leave when the female lead begins to undress? When the talk of the men around you becomes suggestive, do you have the courage to speak up or walk away?

Virtue represents the gravitational pull of goodness. Who has the courage to reject the loose morals of modern culture and stand and live for purity?

All Forms of Impurity Leave a Mark

The world, however, hates purity. All day long we are bombarded by subtle voices telling us that *impurity* is normal, and purity is abnormal if not downright weird. Purity in precious metals, chemical compounds, drugs, medicines, supplements, and scientific experiments is essential. Purity of character in the human soul is ridiculed.

So how does the command "Be pure" impact the decisions you and I will face today? The answer comes in tiny, unseen ways. That's where we are called to walk exampling virtue and planting seeds to change a culture—in regions of life no one sees. Blatant sins of the flesh are self-condemning—adultery, lying, stealing, promiscuity. These need no commentary other than the reminder of Jesus's stark and unyielding command, "Go, and do not sin again."

The command "Be pure" assaults us in smaller doses. The hidden sin, sketchy business deal, flirtatious glance, or off-color comment; the semi-truth, the fudging of an application, the stretching of accuracy, the exaggeration to put oneself in a favorable light; a lust indulged, a suggestive laugh, an ethical boundary pushed to the limit, a whispered curse, an immodest neckline; the grudge nursed, the lurking unforgiveness, the outburst of temper, the inattention to influences of disgusting music and PG-13 films,* the justified untruth—mostly unseen by any other human eye—these build up like scales over spiritual eyesight, dulling vision, preventing the development of God-eyes.

How easily even Christians justify such violations, thinking their impact negligible on character. But a*ll* impurity dulls and blurs the vision—from the dirty joke to the clandestine affair.

It is a sobering truth to realize that in God's eyes causing *another* to sin may be more serious than sinning ourselves.

It's easy to overlook subtleties. Jesus isn't talking about robbing banks. He isn't just talking about dope dealers. He is talking about

---

* Even PG-13 is basically the equivalent of what would have been rated *R* just a few short years ago. Hollywood has lost the virtue-plot almost entirely. We should all be attentive and not mindlessly accept and absorb the evil it churns out.

the unspoken and easily overlooked influence of our lives. We don't usually lead people into sin by dragging them into crime. But we may lead others into sin in ways we never suspect by the laxity of our own obedience.

A child grows up observing the speedometer always inching five or ten miles above the limit and listening to his father mumbling about watching out for cops. Thirty years later a fatal traffic accident can be traced directly back to that careless parental example.

A boy observes his father being more friendly than he should to every pretty woman who crosses his path, sending the boy a wink and a grin as he does. Thirty years later two broken marriages and a string of affairs can be laid like the great millstone at the father's doorstep.

A daughter watches her mother always careful with makeup and perfume, dressing with skirts just a tad high and blouses just a tad low, swimming in the summer in a suit obviously designed to draw eyes. When that same daughter, at eighteen finds herself sinning against the command toward sexual purity, who else but the indiscreet mother can be blamed for tempting her in the directions that led to such sin?

How do the careless words and loose language that fall from our lips invisibly influence those around us? If it is a sin to take God's name in vain by punctuating our speech with, "Oh God" every five minutes, and if those who are watching adopt the same habit, what other conclusion can be drawn but that we have "led them into sin"? What does the full example of my life say to a watching world? It should be very sobering that another may be led into sin from something I say or do.

Christians are a *watched* people.

But we are lazy. We drift from our foundations. We have to keep aware of spiritual rudders. These are the priorities and perspectives that keep life's ship on course, moving straight and true. What are our *deepest* foundations? What principles and truths set the tone for our life's outlook? We need to look in the mirror daily. Is my hand on the rudder? Am I moving in the direction I want to go? Is God *pleased* with the way I am steering my ship?

It is easy to deflect such questions with generalizations. But spiritualizations don't grow us into whole, sound, and *pure* men and women.

A Nation's Slide into Moral Depravity

We've noted that Leviticus 18 reveals how seriously God takes sexual purity. As personal as purity is, the Levitical law was written to a nation. These were not mere personal laws; they were *national* laws. It was "against the law" to engage in forbidden sexual activity.

Though younger Americans may not even know this, not so long ago adultery, abortion, and homosexuality were against the law in the United States. Recently I was stunned to be reminded of the speed with which the progressive tidal wave of unvirtue has swept upon us. In a television legal drama I was watching, filmed in the year 2000, a fifteen-year-old girl was arrested for murder, for killing her unborn child in its seventh month. A short twenty-three years later, now laws are being passed allowing murder up to the moment of birth, and babies who survive are "terminated" outside the womb.

As horrifying as it is, abortion does not represent the *source* of the problem. That problem is sex outside marriage leading to unwanted pregnancies. It is not only that premarital sex is commonplace; it is that our culture considers it normal. *That* is the travesty. The illicit sexual relations that are hateful to God are considered so normal that no one asks if "pro-choice" might reasonably include the *choice* not to sin sexually. Teens are taught to have "protected sex" rather than taught the virtue of true *choice*—choosing *not* to sin. Christian parents who go along with it are essentially teaching their children *how to sin*.

Sex outside marriage *isn't* considered a sin anymore. So we'll make sure pro-choice excludes that all important choice. The choice *not* to engage in sex is off the table. It is assumed to be so normal that personal choice doesn't even come into it.

Such is a national disgrace. Not only the *result*—abortion—but also the *cause*—sexual promiscuity. It is more than a disgrace; it is an abomination against purity. The free sex libertinism of the sixties has gone mainstream.

Everyone knows these abominations are wrong. What does former Penn State intercollegiate swimmer Will Thomas think in his heart of hearts in the small hours of the night? He *knows* that pretending his name is Lia Catherine is a gigantic con. He knows it as well as everyone else. When he's alone, do tears come to his eyes at what he has done to himself? Or does he silently smile at the gullibility of the liberal world to embrace the illusion? What will he do years from now when the Spirit of God gets its hold on him, and he realizes he wants to be a husband and a father and a *whole* man of integrity? How many such bitter and guiltful awakenings will there be from the evils the myriad LGBTQ falsehoods have forced upon the world?*

All the while Washington stands on the sidelines and cheers Will Thomas as a boy/girl of courage rather than a troubled youth in desperate need of psychological counseling. If ever we needed integrity from our leaders, it is in addressing the crisis of promiscuity of our times.

But if leaders have so abandoned reason as to legalize same-sex marriage and teach transgenderism to elementary school children, what's the big deal in sex outside marriage? It's tame by comparison on the depravity-meter.

Promiscuity is always one of the sure signs that a nation is on the way down. As the moral fiber goes, so goes the integrity and strength of a people.

And Washington, DC, and fifty statehouses are asleep.

How many does it take to change a culture? It takes one who turns away and says, "The world may laugh at my old-fashioned values, but I will be pure. Nor will I rob another of *their* purity."

---

* Will Thomas, men's NCAA swimmer for Penn State in 2019–20, changed his name to Lia Catherine, and subsequently enjoyed a record-breaking career on the women's Penn State swim team, winning the Division 1 national championship in the women's five-hundred-yard freestyle.

24

HONOR
the unvirtue: dishonor

The old, hard totalitarianism had a vision for the world that required
the eradication of Christianity. The new, soft totalitarianism does too,
and we are not equipped to resist its sneakier attack.

— Rod Dreher

We tend to think of the Old Testament Levitical law as little more than legalistic do's and don'ts that have little bearing on our lives. Some of its regulations, however, are surprisingly relevant.

The Honor Chapter

Take Leviticus 19, for example, the chapter following God's commands concerning sexual purity. Read through this list from the New International Version. Surely we would be better citizens, and the United States a better country, by following these national laws of ancient Israel.

Coming on the heels of the sexual purity chapter, this could be called the "honor chapter"—honor parents, strangers, the poor, your neighbor, the deaf and blind, your daughter, your workers; honor justice, honesty, truth, property—with a few miscellaneous commands thrown in.

- "Respect your mother and father" (v. 3a).
- "When you reap the harvest of your land, do not reap to the very edges of your field or gather the gleanings of your harvest.

Do not go over your vineyard a second time or pick up the grapes that have fallen. Leave them for the poor and the foreigner" (vv. 9–10a).

- "Do not steal" (v. 11a).
- "Do not lie" (v. 11b).
- "Do not deceive one another" (v. 11c).
- "Do not defraud or rob your neighbor" (v. 13a).
- "Do not hold back the wages of a hired worker" (v. 13b).
- "Do not pervert justice" (v. 15a).
- "Do not show partiality to the poor or favoritism to the great, but judge your neighbor fairly" (v. 15b).
- "Do not go about spreading slander among your people" (v. 16a).
- "Do not do anything that endangers your neighbor's life" (v. 16b).
- "Do not seek revenge or bear a grudge against anyone among your people" (v. 18a).
- "Love your neighbor as yourself" (v. 18b).
- "Do not practice divination or seek omens" (v. 26b).
- "Do not put tattoo marks on yourselves" (v. 28b).
- "Do not degrade your daughter by making her a prostitute, or the land will . . . be filled with wickedness" (v. 29).
- "Do not turn to mediums or seek out spiritists, for you will be defiled by them" (v. 31).
- "Do not use dishonest standards when measuring length, weight, or quantity" (v. 35).
- "Use honest scales and honest weights" (v. 36a).

One of the verses I find most fascinating is found in Leviticus 19:32: "Stand up in the presence of the aged, show respect for the elderly and revere your God" (NIV).

This down-to-earth practicality is astonishing to read. In today's culture, youth rules. Our entire society centers around the young. Imagine if it were an unwritten code that everyone followed! *Rise respectfully when an old man or woman walks into the room.*

Bloodline Not Virtue

In Old Testament times, this injunction from Leviticus 19:32 was more than only an unwritten code; it was a *national law.* The idea is beyond comprehension—what if the U.S. Congress passed a law, upheld by the Supreme Court, that all elderly men and women were to be shown deference and honor wherever they went, their words listened to respectfully whenever they spoke? It is hardly even necessary to mention how differently our culture functions.

Honor of parents, grandparents, forebears, and their legacy is found throughout the Old Testament. The fascinating heart of these oft-repeated commands is this: Honor was not commanded because a given man or woman or father or grandfather was necessarily an *honorable* person. Some were; some weren't. Honor was commanded, period.

Honor was commanded toward the good *and* the bad. Honor was commanded not because any of them were perfect, or good people at all, but because they came before. Their blood and legacy flowed into and through their descendants. It was the legacy of their *bloodline* that was to be honored, not the virtue of their character. If they happened to have lived virtuous lives, so much the better. But that was not the basis for honor.

My forebears' blood is *in* me and in our nation. I am to honor them for that. I honor them because I am alive.

Honor is not based on virtue but on honor for the past—*because* it is *my* past.

Modernity has turned all this upside-down. Modernity says that we are no longer required to honor anyone whom we consider dishonorable. If we don't like them, we don't have to honor them.

The entire culture shouts at children from the day they are born to *dishonor* their parents. No wonder so many young people enter the teen years full of rebellion and independence. Flexing their teen muscles, they are but living out the lies of unvirtue society has fed into them all their lives.

National Honor

The national application I find embedded in this ancient Old Testament command may be unexpected. The crisis of parental and elder dishonor is a major factor in the success of progressivism's anti-authority agenda. The epidemic of anti-male and anti-father dishonor in our time—condoned and encouraged by the feminist Left—is indeed a national travesty.

There exists, however, a related and more general virtue that is in equal danger. Its destruction lies at the heart of the progressive agenda. That is *honor of our nation's historic past.* Along with its attempted eradication of many traditional virtues, progressivism has systematically repudiated much of what has come before in U.S. history. Rather than rise in respect to the past, its agenda cries, "Cut off all ties to the past. Rebel against bad parents and bad leaders, against white bigoted racist historical figures, against our entire history. Strike them from the obelisks. Remove them from the history books, for they were evil. Do *not* honor the past. Revise and rewrite our history to reflect white Christian racism not exceptionalism."

All this is a sinister falsehood based on the reverse-racism of progressivism's anti-Christian, anti-white agenda. Roots are more than memories. Roots contain the lifeblood of any organism. There is no life without a root system. Progressivism, however, wants to *sever* all our spiritual, cultural, and historical roots.

We return to the heart of the biblical command: honor that is not based on virtue. It is required because the blood that flows from the past gives life to the future. The national lifeblood of our country has come down through our history and its men and women. That history is to be given its due because it is *our* history. Rustlers *and* sheriffs, Indians *and* cowboys, blacks *and* whites, good people *and* bad people, plantation owners *and* slaves, rich *and* poor, Abraham Lincoln *and* Robert E. Lee—*every* one is part of our living root system. We do not honor evil, but neither do we pretend that certain parts of our history never happened or rewrite history with revisionist theories that have no basis in historical fact.

Honor has nothing to do with whether George Washington or Thomas Jefferson owned slaves. They were men of their times. Our history was not a perfect history. No nation's is. Nations mature through growing pains.

Writer Dayton Duncan put it into perspective this way, speaking of America's national parks:

> The Declaration of Independence began with this incredible statement, that all men, all human beings, are created equal. We will be chasing that ideal, those words, for the rest of our history, often too slowly, never quite reaching it, even yet. But that's the statement we're chasing . . . . Like the notion of freedom, we've always been arguing over it, we've always been trying to grapple with its meaning, and always trying to, on the one hand remain true to the ideal, but leaving it up to each succeeding generation to either push it a little bit farther, or broaden it a little bit more.*

Thus we decry and correct the abuses as history and enlightenment advance. Along with that, we can equally extol the virtues of our history. No one will argue that there is little virtue to be found in our national disgrace of slavery or the national travesty of our Civil War. Yet fast-forwarding 150 years, no country on the planet contains as much black wealth or offers as much opportunity for the descendants of those mistreated slaves. That does not justify the evil of slavery, but we have to live in the present. How many of those who demand *ex post facto* reparations from white America for the sufferings of their great-great-great grandparents wish they had been born in Somalia, Niger, or Liberia or would consider going back to them now with their national standard of living? With the bad has come good. That

---

* Ken Burns, "Great Nature," *The National Parks*, episode 5 (Florentine Films and WETA Television, 2009). This film series is so excellent it should be shown in every school. Its perspective of U.S. history, and the American family, is so much more healthy and accurate than much of what passes for American history today.

does not excuse the bad but yet offers a historic balance to a complex picture of national growth.*

We are all—whites, blacks, Native Americans, the descendants of Chinese slaves, rich and poor alike—indebted to the advantages of our history of American exceptionalism, even as we cut off the branches that grew as suckers and viruses on the tree of that exceptionalism. We are all linked to a common root system that has, all of us taken together, given us life. Pruning off some of the branches is necessary for continued health, but cutting down the tree is a singularly foolish way to accomplish it.

Judy's and my ancestries both contain outlaws along with wonderful examples of spirituality. Our ancestries are a mixed potpourri of good and bad. Judy's Cherokee ancestors were removed from North Carolina to Oklahoma on the infamous Trail of Tears. For all I know, some of my Oklahoma relatives may have participated in that travesty. The Trail of Tears is, for Cherokees, as emblematic of white cruelty as slavery is for blacks. But does Judy hate white America for the Trail of Tears? Does she hold *me* responsible for the suffering of her Cherokee forebears?

These are obviously inane questions even to raise. Yet it is precisely this reasoning that is rewriting U.S. history and is now teaching an entirely false revisionism to America's youth based on critical race theory. Judy does not despise white America for the Trail of Tears. We both love and revere her Cherokee roots no less than we do our Quaker roots. Those combined root systems have merged and grown together to produce life. I don't hold scalped white settlers against the whole race of Native Americans, including Judy's ancestors, any more than she holds it against me and all whites for the Trail of Tears. There is a level of maturity required to understand history, which is often lacking in progressivism's rush to rewrite the past.

---

* As in everything we are discussing, I am speaking to large principles. Red-herring exceptions exist suitable for distracting from the point if such is what anyone wants to do. Hitler and Nazi Germany are a different case than George Washington and Thomas Jefferson. Germany must come to terms with its more recent past with a different kind of repentance than America does even in the matter of slavery. Nazism cannot be explained on the basis of historic growing pains.

American exceptionalism is a sweeping symphony, with movements in minor keys containing strains of uncomfortable dissonance running through them. But that still-being-written symphony is one of the most triumphant national and historic symphonies ever written. It is worthy of remembrance and honor, worthy to be played in elementary schools and high schools and colleges and universities across the land. Those who want to take the manuscripts of that symphony and burn them and replace them with a street concert of discordant rap, would do well to reflect what happens to growing things when they are cut off from their roots.

The Trail of Tears and cruel whites who enforced it, outlaws on both sides of our family tree, Quakers and honorable men and women of God also on both sides, good and bad women and men—Judy and I honor our joint past because it is *our* past. We are proud of it, not because it was all good but because the man and woman we are emerged out of it.

I was reared in the small college town of Arcata in northern California. My father owned a small photography business on Arcata's central plaza. Almost daily I saw the statue of President William McKinley rising from the pedestal at its center across the street from the shop that was my second home. Intrinsic to Arcata's heritage, the image of the assassinated president stood as a silent reminder that we are a country with *presidents*, not kings or dictators, but also a nation with bad people in it who do bad things and sometimes even kill presidents.* It was a balanced and healthy message for Arcata's youth to be reminded of.

That statue is now gone, toppled some years ago by hot-headed college students in the wave of progressive revisionism that swept through the country. As far as I know, President McKinley's only crime against American history was that he was white. I cannot see that Arcata is any better off without this reminder of one of our nation's obscure presidents who contributed to the national bloodline of our root system.

---

* Republican President William McKinley was assassinated by an anarchist in 1901.

It is a strange nation indeed that cuts off its roots and foolishly considers itself stronger as a result.

25

SILENCE
the unvirtue: talkativeness

*Preserve grace in silence. You will be more glad that
you have kept silence than that you have talked much.*
— Thomas à Kempis

Many no doubt began this reading assuming it would outline a strategy for loudly proclaiming truth to our culture, attempting to turn America back to its roots by forceful arguments, perceptively delivered by media, ballot, and personal persuasion.

The Order of Ecclesiastes 3:7

Ecclesiastes 3 begins, "For everything there is a season," and there is certainly a time to speak. Those times, however, may not be as frequent or as automatic as we think. The Ecclesiastes also reminds us that there is a time to keep silent. This chapter highlights the truth that silence, counterintuitive as it may seem, may often be a more potent tool in our arsenal in the ideological war than the bullhorn, the sandwich board, or the pundit's microphone.

In the present culture of unending and vociferous debate, the first half of Ecclesiastes 3:7b is usually glossed over ("a time to keep silence") so that the second phrase can shout forth with all the subtlety of a hundred-piece brass band:

AND A TIME TO SPEAK!

The order of the phrases is imperative: "a time to keep silence, and a time to speak."

- It may be that silence paves the way for speaking.
- It may be that silence tills the soil for the fertile receiving of word-seeds.
- It may be that silence opens doors and windows of receptivity.
- It may be that words spoken hastily and *not* in their proper season may slam shut those doors and windows.

Conveying truth is double-sided. Both mouth and ears are required. In a shouting match, no one hears anything. All mouths are open; all ears are closed. Truth can't get in.

The futility of trying to drown out everyone else is obvious. We *know* it accomplishes nothing. Yet we all persist in that futility. It may in fact be *silence* that will lead the way toward truth more subtly than an increase in volume. Preserving grace in silence occasionally enables others to hear their own illogic. Foolishness may more effectively be combated with a silent mirror held up to its folly than trying in vain to shout it down.

Kempis on Silence

The evils inherent in many forms of talkativeness are obvious: gossip, slander, criticism, innuendo. Yet simply talking *too much*, even when not spreading untruth and falsehood, indicates a character weakness. Lack of self-control, preoccupation with self, and insensitivity toward others are glaringly on display in the individual who simply can't keep his or her mouth shut.

Many others have emphasized the importance of holding the tongue. Thomas à Kempis speaks of it more eloquently in his *The Imitation of Christ* than anyone I know.

- Be not wise in your own conceit.
- Do not be too confident in your own opinion.

- Do not busy yourself with the words and deeds of others.
- Do not be idle or spend your time in talk.
- Withdraw from speaking vainly and gadding idly.
- Diligently attend unto yourself and keep silent concerning others.
- Consider what you are within you, and give no heed to the many whisperings of this world.
- Listen not to the voices sounding without, but for the Truth teaching inwardly.
- Walk inwardly and do not be moved with every wind of fleeting words.
- Preserve grace in silence.
- Allow the Lord to teach you without noise of words, confusion of opinions, ambitions of honor, or the scuffling of arguments.
- Be not therefore too confident in your own opinion, but be willing to hear the judgment of others.
- Often I wish that I had held my peace sooner than I have spoken.
- We very willingly talk of those things which we most love or desire, and often, alas! in vain, and to no purpose.
- If it be lawful and expedient for you to speak, speak those things that may edify.
- You will be more glad that you have kept silence, than that you have talked much.
- To be able to live peaceably with hard and perverse persons, or with the disorderly, or with such as go contrary to us, is a great grace, and a most commendable and manly thing.
- You will never be thus inwardly religious, unless you pass over other men's affairs with silence, and look especially to yourself.
- Keep yourself gently at peace.
- It is no small prudence to keep silence in an evil time.
- O how good is it and tending to peace, to be silent about other men.[1]

An Unproven Conviction

I can offer no logical reason for the point of this chapter. With everything within us we *desperately* want to shout out the convincing arguments for our points of view. We *must* tell people where they are wrong! We are *compelled* to expose the folly and illogic of our opinion-opponents with persuasive and forceful arguments.

I have no cogent argument of my own to bolster my conviction that the blaring brass band tactic will never change the world. The Trump-rally approach may get some results in the short term. But it will never provide a foundation toward a permanent solution for what ails this country as the train of progressivism speeds toward the cliff of its destiny.

I can offer no provable rationale for virtuous, gracious, gentlemanly soft-spokenness as a more effective strategy other than to say, "Try it. Experiment and see if over time—and time is one of the necessary components of the Kempis strategy—a few people don't begin listening to your quiet, thoughtful, well-seasoned, and gracious words more attentively when you follow the order of Ecclesiastes 3:7 and lead with the virtue of silence."

Maybe you will not find the Kempis strategy helpful. I am well aware that gracious listening does *not* open doors and windows in everyone. There are several individuals with whom I have been attempting this listening strategy for years, and they remain as loquacious, long winded, and opinionated as ever.

Yet I remain convinced that megaphones and soapboxes will not succeed in planting truth-seeds into the heart of progressivism's gullibly unthinking disciples. I can only say, "Try an alternate strategy. Give it time. Be patient in allowing quiet and humble virtue to do its work. Then see what may result."

You may not change the world by yourself. But remember that future senator who may be watching.

Virtue is our best weapon. In truth, it is our *only* weapon. As you engage with the world in the commitment to live not by lies, it is a supreme virtue to preserve grace in silence.

26

WISDOM
the unvirtue: foolishness

The beginning of wisdom is this: Get wisdom,
and whatever you get, get insight.
— Proverbs 4:7

The perceptive reader will have noticed by now that the virtues we have discussed are of many diverse kinds. Nor has there been an attempt to carry out an exhaustive study of the subject of virtue. We have focused mostly on those of particular national and cultural importance for men and women of virtue to reclaim the historic principles of America's roots.

Momentary Virtue and Lifelong Virtue

Some virtues can be practiced anytime, anywhere by anyone in any circumstance.

Acts of kindness may be momentary single events or lifestyle patterns. Even a murderer can stop, help a lady who has fallen back to her feet, and offer a kind word and a smile, but then not do another kind thing for a year—or never again at all. Kindness is not dependent on character; it is only dependent on kindness though being an individual of character certainly increases the likelihood of kindness being regular and frequent expressions of that character. Many of the virtues are like this. Anyone can practice them at anytime. Even a timid milquetoast may rise to the occasion with an unexpected act of bravery and courage.

Other virtues, however, go deeper. They are virtues of lifelong selflessness, humility, and strength of personhood. The virtue of "virtue" is obviously like this. Being a man or woman of virtue— a *virtuous* man or woman—requires a lifelong orientation of personal dedication to goodness, selflessness, kindness, and moral character. It takes ten thousand individual *moments* of virtue to build the foundation of a virtuous character able to withstand the tests of life when they come.

Integrity is another virtue of lifelong character orientation. It is not deepened within personhood in a day nor a year. Ten years may be enough for integrity to send out a few shoots. The roots may have been stretching down unseen for years, but the fruit is slow-growing, gradually expanding and flourishing over a lifetime of choices and attitudes.

Other virtues combine both the momentary and the lifelong. Honor and respect may be shown in acts of respect (rising in the presence of the aged) yet may (or may not) arise out of a deep and abiding honor toward all men and women that extends deep into the marrow of an individual's character.

Wisdom: The Crown of Virtue

Approaching the end of our exploration of virtue as it impacts not only the *people* we are but also the fiber of the *nation* we are collectively making of ourselves, we arrive at perhaps the deepest of all the lifetime virtues. Wisdom probes to the very core of personhood and, like a mighty oak, grows (*if* it grows) stronger and more evident over a lifetime. There are few wise twenty-years-olds, perhaps a few more beginning-to-be-wise forty-year-olds. But wisdom in the human family is generally clustered toward the end of life's spectrum.

A lifetime being a so-called good person, even a lifetime of virtue and integrity, does not ensure that wisdom will emerge out of these character traits. Wisdom is of an altogether different kind than the rest of the virtues. It is the summit, the completion of all the virtues—in George MacDonald's colorful words, "the topmost stone set on with rejoicing"—hopefully the fulfillment of a life well-lived, the crown of a long obedience in the same direction.

Wisdom, too, is a word whose understanding benefits from a brief look at Webster: "The right use of knowledge; the choice of laudable ends, and of the best means to accomplish them. . . . [T]he faculty of discerning or judging what is most just, proper and useful . . . . *[P]ractical wisdom* is nearly synonymous with *discretion*. It differs somewhat from *prudence*, in this respect; *prudence* is the exercise of sound judgment in avoiding evils; *wisdom* is the exercise of sound judgment either in avoiding evils or attempting good."[1]

Yet not even a lifetime of virtue automatically produces wisdom. Wisdom grows in a different soil than all other aspects of personal character. That unique and special soil must be sought, sought diligently as a great treasure, then cultivated, nurtured, and tended carefully. Nothing about wisdom is automatic. Not even many years of good habits and good choices will produce it. They help toward it, but they are not the thing itself. The other virtues are like soil additives to aid wisdom's growth, but the essential soil itself is of another kind.

God's Eyes

The soil of wisdom is the outlook and perspective of God. Wisdom is therefore essentially spiritual in nature.

We come into this world capable of thinking of nothing but ourselves—our own needs and desires. Some people never progress beyond that stage all their lives. The tree of wisdom can find no soil in which to grow. The lives even of virtuous men and women may yet be oriented through the outlook of their *own* eyesight, their *own* predispositions, their *own* biases and experiences. They may be good, virtuous, kind, humble people who are yet seeing all of life only through their *own* eyes.

On the other hand, those who set their minds and hearts to see life and the world, other people and themselves, through the lens of *God's* purposes, not their own, gradually begin—faintly at first—to see through his eyes. A completely different kind of eyesight develops that is utterly unknown to the secular world. Even to attempt to explain it to a secularist would be pointless.

This is a *sought* perspective. We have to *look* for it, *seek* it, make this new and unfamiliar kind of eyesight a lifelong quest. It is not easy to lay aside our own perspectives and set out to discover God's outlook. It is not natural to the independent, self-focused human spirit. But when one seeks that alternative way of seeing, the purposes of God slowly come into focus. Over a lifetime the tree of wisdom grows.

It may begin in the twenties, maybe in the thirties, and for some not until later. Wherever the germ of wisdom finds a home, and its seeds are planted in wisdom's soil and are then watered and nurtured through quietude, humility, virtue, and choices in the right direction, they send roots deep. *God-sight* grows as the tree of wisdom grows, sending out its branches and leaves into the world of God's revelation.

Dedicating oneself to discovering the nature and character of God, to knowing and understanding his purposes, then falling in with those purposes as God's man or woman, will seem to many like an incomprehensible life objective. Yet such is the path to wisdom.

Wisdom, then, may be described as seeing life, the world, oneself, and others to the extent our humanity allows—as Paul phrases it, through a glass darkly—as God sees them, with *his* outlook and perspective, with *his* eternal purposes shining out behind them.

How to Grow Wisdom—Seek It, Cry Out for It . . . Get It!

The biblical book of Proverbs has a single theme: wisdom.

In the following passages, we find the secret of wisdom unlocked. It must be sought for the treasure it is. It comes from God, and he will give it. Once planted, the tree of wisdom flourishes in the garden of integrity, uprightness, righteousness, knowledge, and discretion. Therefore, Solomon urges, spare no effort: "Get wisdom."

> My son, if you receive my words and treasure up my
> commandments with you, making your ear attentive
> to wisdom and inclining your heart to understanding;

yes, if you cry out for insight and raise your voice for understanding, if you seek it like silver and search for it as for hidden treasures; then you will understand the fear of the LORD and find the knowledge of God. For the LORD gives wisdom; from his mouth come knowledge and understanding; he stores up sound wisdom for the upright; he is a shield to those who walk in integrity. . . . Then you will understand righteousness and justice and equity, every good path; for wisdom will come into your heart, and knowledge will be pleasant to your soul; discretion will watch over you; understanding will guard you. (2:1–7, 9–11)

Happy is the man who finds wisdom, and the man who gets understanding, for the gain from it is better than gain from silver and its profit better than gold. She is more precious than jewels, and nothing you desire can compare with her. . . . Her ways are ways of pleasantness, and all her paths are peace. (3:13–15, 17)

Get wisdom; get insight. Do not forsake her, and she will keep you; love her, and she will guard you. (4:5–6)

The beginning of wisdom is this: Get wisdom, and whatever you get, get insight. (4:7)

We would not be told in the book of Proverbs to seek wisdom so diligently, as if for hidden treasure, if it were not possible to find it. That we are told to *seek* it reveals that we *can* find it. It is therefore no magical, ethereal, airy phantom—wisdom is down-to-earth, practical, attainable. Those who seek it and find it over a lifetime will be richly rewarded.

And yet, seeing life and ourselves, especially other people, through the lens of God's purposes is the most unnatural thing in the world. Independence and pride, our natural rebellion, and an entire life spent trying to get our own way, all work against it. Learning to get our eyes off ourselves and pointed in another direction is the most difficult assignment we have been given in life.

Virtue assists in this lifetime search. It trains our eyes in habits of goodness and truth and integrity. Practicing the virtues helps us see as God sees.*

Do We Care Enough about Wisdom to Return to Founding Truths?

Spiritual in nature though it may be, wisdom is more practical than it may first appear. Most of the national conundrums we have talked about that sit squarely in the bull's-eye of the current national debate would be put to rest instantly if our national leaders and the people of the country were seeking wisdom.

Wisdom answers everything because seeing through God's eyes answers everything. Nearly any issue one brings to the table is clarified instantly through the eyes of wisdom vs. foolishness—abortion, homosexuality, same-sex marriage, racism, injustice, unkindness, adultery, divorce, and even an issue such as immigration.

What does God think about unkindness?

What does God think about abortion?

What does seeing through God's eyes tell us about racism of *all* kinds—about the racism of BLM toward whites no less than the racism that caused slavery and the Trail of Tears?

Sadly, wisdom is not to be found in great supply in Washington, DC. Our nation's leaders are looking through their own eyes, through the eyes of their party, through the eyes of wealth and power, through the eyes of political correctness, though the eyes of liberalism and conservatism. Wisdom cannot grow in the soil of opinionated agendas.

God's eyes look far beyond human opinions and agendas to high Truth. Where are those with courage and understanding to see through God's eyes, those who will lead our country in the ways of wisdom?

---

* For more on some of the practicalities of wisdom, see appendix 3.

In the United States of America, the purposes of God send us straight back to the Bible, the truths of Christianity, and the founding principles of our nation.

Returning to the importance of mentors, though I never met him personally in this life, I will now turn to consider a man in whom I believe the years grew a courageous wisdom and whose legacy and example I hope lasts many years into the future. He was not a perfect man. He was a man with flaws in spite of the dubious doctrine of infallibility. But in the same humanness we all share, he was a man of God, whose example tells us much about the ideological war in which we are engaged.

27

A Prophetic Shepherd's Courage

> We are building a dictatorship of relativism that does not
> recognize anything as definitive and whose ultimate goal
> consists solely of one's own ego and desires.
> — Cardinal Joseph Ratzinger

Two transformative personalities rose to prominence on the world stage almost simultaneously eighteen years ago at the time of this writing.

One would change the trajectory of American culture and hence the ethical, moral, racial, and political direction of the entire planet.

The other would not.

Both were transformational but for opposite reasons. One was awarded the Nobel Peace Prize, though the dark side of his legacy may point to his having encouraged division, racial hatred, disregard for law, the repudiation of Western Christian ethic, the vilification of America's history, and for giving his tacit approval to an explosion of hedonism throughout the nation. Yet in spite of these rarely voiced consequences of his rise to power, he was hailed as one of the world's most beloved men.

The other was quietly exiled to live out his final years in ignominy, the legacy of his courage swept under the carpet where, it was hoped, it would be forgotten in the wave of popularity of his liberal successor. His was the eternal legacy of a prophetic shepherd's courage that the world was incapable of seeing but will never be forgotten.

The year was 2005.

In January of that year, Barack Obama was first sworn in as U.S. senator. He was immediately earmarked for higher things.

Three months later, on April 19, Cardinal Joseph Ratzinger became Pope Benedict XVI. He had the day before given a brief homily during the Vatican mass. In it, embedded within remarks about several passages of the New Testament, the man who would the next day become pope drew a line in the sand, setting himself against the modernity and progressivism of the age. The challenge was brief. But there was no mistaking its intent, as his subsequent writings and forceful words against modernism revealed. He had sealed his fate even before donning the pontifical robes.

A Historic Speech on Behalf of Virtue

I may be reading too much cosmic import into the unfolding of events. However, sometimes those involved in circumstances on the earthly plane do not fully apprehend their significance in the eternal realm. I truly perceive a high import to these events, perhaps even more than Benedict himself appreciated at the time. In him I recognize the prophetic example of a true shepherd of the church attempting to challenge his people to stand for virtue, tradition, and truth against the world.

He was a modern-day "Benedict" who joined with the sixth-century St. Benedict of Nursia in calling true believers, in Paul's words in 2 Corinthians 6:17, to "come out from them, and be separate."

The former pope was an example to the clergy worldwide—pastors and priests and ministers and lay leaders and teachers in every church and denomination. He exemplified the challenge of all God's men and women to stand tall, to resist the world, and to exhort their people to stand for truth and "live not by lies." He was, for all of us, a profound living example of the virtue of courage.

For that reason, we are devoting this chapter to this contemporary Benedict. Doing so ties together not only the theme of endangered virtues but is also linked to my fictional series Tribulation Cult, one of the subplots of which centers around a secret document called "The Benedict Brief."

That Pope Benedict was a Catholic and German I find fascinating and significant. I am neither. My upbringing was evangelical, so taking Pope Benedict as one of the primary and forceful examples of virtue in our time is therefore wonderfully fitting as identifying this important message as one for *all* Christians across the spectrum—and for *all* the world.

How appropriate that this clarion call against the progressivism of our time came from a native of Germany, where the Reformation began, and where, according to Francis Schaeffer, the beginning of the end of absolutes and the rise of modern progressivism also began. Here was a new German, standing in the tradition of Luther, as I referenced in the introduction, saying, "Here I stand." Thus Cardinal Joseph Ratzinger nailed his version of the "Ninety-Five Theses" on his own Wittenberg Door at the mass at the Vatican Basilica on April 18, 2005.

The following represents a little less than half of that full homily. I glean enormous significance from his opening, quoting Jesus's "first public sermon," so to speak, in Nazareth from Luke 4. Jesus speaks of announcing a new year of the Lord and adds, "Today this scripture has been fulfilled in your hearing." Cardinal Ratzinger was too humble to compare himself with Jesus, yet he boldly proclaimed, "Christ's mandate has become our mandate." He was sufficiently aware of history to recognize his unique position as the first new pope of the third millennium. It is not too much to imagine himself likewise hoping to announce that a new day was also coming to the church. From what follows, it is clear what he meant that new day to imply—a church standing courageously against the evils and relativism of the times.

As Cardinal Ratzinger gradually built upon that beginning, the climactic moment for which the speech will forever after be known, came with his identification of a "dictatorship of relativism." It was a powerful and controversial phrase—a direct challenge thrown in progressivism's face.

The terms sprinkled through the speech are unmistakable. They continue that challenge: *trivialization of evil, liberalism, ideological currents, ways of thinking, atheism, agnosticism, error, deceit from truth, deception,* and *syncretism.* He called on Christians everywhere to "mature adult faith." He does so also exhorting Christian leaders: "We must develop this adult faith; we must guide the flock of Christ to this faith." The latter word *syncretism* is especially significant. Literally, the word means "combining." In theological use it means combining and merging different beliefs, even *contradictory* ideas, by seeking a synthesis or underlying unity between them. This allows an inclusive approach where there is no right or wrong—the very foundation of relativism.

The soon-to-be pope was drawing that line in the sand. Like his Master, he was called to proclaim truth. He never condoned syncretic progressivism.

Let us hear him from that pivotal day.

> At this moment of great responsibility, let us listen with special attention to what the Lord says to us in his own words. . . .
>
> The Messiah, speaking of himself, says that he was sent "to announce a year of favour from the Lord and a day of vindication by our God" ([Isaiah] 61:2). . . .
>
> Christ's mandate has become our mandate through the priestly anointing. We are called to proclaim . . . .
>
> Christ's mercy is not a grace that comes cheap, nor does it imply the trivialization of evil. . . .
>
> Let us move on to the second reading, the letter to the Ephesians. . . .
>
> Let us dwell on only two points. The first is the journey towards "the maturity of Christ," as the Italian text says, simplifying it slightly. More precisely, in accordance with the Greek text, we should speak of the "measure of the

fullness of Christ" that we are called to attain if we are to be true adults in the faith. We must not remain children in faith, in the condition of minors. And what does it mean to be children in faith? St Paul answers: it means being "tossed here and there, carried about by every wind of doctrine" ([Ephesians] 4:14). This description is very timely!

How many winds of doctrine have we known in recent decades, how many ideological currents, how many ways of thinking. The small boat of the thought of many Christians has often been tossed about by these waves— flung from one extreme to another: from Marxism to liberalism, even to libertinism; from collectivism to radical individualism; from atheism to a vague religious mysticism; from agnosticism to syncretism and so forth. Every day new sects spring up, and what St. Paul says about human deception and the trickery that strives to entice people into error (cf. [Ephesians] 4:14) comes true.

Today, having a clear faith based on the Creed of the Church is often labeled as fundamentalism. Whereas relativism, that is, letting oneself be "tossed here and there, carried about by every wind of doctrine," seems the only attitude that can cope with modern times. We are building a dictatorship of relativism that does not recognize anything as definitive and whose ultimate goal consists solely of one's own ego and desires.

We, however, have a different goal: the Son of God, the true man. He is the measure . . . . An "adult" faith is not a faith that follows the trends of fashion and the latest novelty; a mature adult faith is deeply rooted in friendship with Christ. It is this friendship that opens us up to all that is good and gives us a criterion by which to distinguish the true from the false, and deceit from truth.

We must develop this adult faith; we must guide the flock of Christ to this faith. . . .

On this theme, St. Paul offers us as a fundamental formula for Christian existence some beautiful words, in contrast to the continual vicissitudes of those who, like children, are tossed about by the waves: make truth in love. Truth and love coincide in Christ. . . .

Let us now look at the Gospel, from whose riches I would like to draw only two small observations. The Lord addresses these wonderful words to us: "I no longer speak of you as slaves. . . . Instead, I call you friends" ([John] 15:15). . . .

[T]he Lord calls us friends, . . . He entrusts his Body, the Church, to us.

To our weak minds, to our weak hands, he entrusts his truth . . . .

Thank you, Jesus, for your friendship! . . .

We have received the faith to give it to others—we are priests in order to serve others. And we must bear fruit that will endure. . . .

The fruit that endures is therefore all that we have sown in human souls: love, knowledge, a gesture capable of touching hearts, words that open the soul to joy in the Lord. So let us go and pray to the Lord to help us bear fruit that endures. . . .

At this time . . . let us above all pray insistently to the Lord that after his great gift of Pope John Paul II, he will once again give us a Pastor according to his own heart, a Pastor who will guide us to knowledge of Christ, to his love and to true joy. Amen.

The day after speaking these words, Cardinal Ratzinger became Pope Benedict XVI. In spite of this stirring beginning, he was to last less than eight years.

Result of a Shepherd's Courage

The new pope's challenge to progressivism was strong and forceful.

In the very year of his election, Benedict approved a Vatican document instructing that the church "cannot admit to the seminary or to holy orders those who practice homosexuality, present deep-seated homosexual tendencies or support the so-called 'gay culture.' Such persons, in fact, find themselves in a situation that gravely hinders them from relating correctly to men and women."

This is an explosive statement. What other major public leader in the past twenty years had the courage to say for all the world to hear: *Those who support the gay culture cannot relate correctly to men and women.*

Predictably, progressivism fought back. It was soon obvious that Benedict was unsatisfactory to Catholicism's liberal elite. Sadly, the future of Catholicism followed the example of the United States, not the challenge of Benedict. The United States had chosen to go in a *very* different direction!

Barack Obama was elected U.S. president in 2008 and received the Nobel Peace Prize in 2009.

The new pope realized that his clarion call would not, as Luther's, end in a new Reformation of truth and a return to the ancient and founding truths of Christendom. He bowed to the multitude of pressures being mounted against him and resigned in quiet though unspoken humiliation in 2013—the first pope to resign in six hundred years.

It is generally known that he was virtually compelled to step down. The reason often cited behind the scenes is that he had been ineffective in dealing with the ongoing sex abuse issues of the church, a charge that extended back to his years as a cardinal in Germany. The abuse scandal, his academic personality being "out of touch" with the needs of the times, and his inability to act as a strong leader over the disputatious Vatican hierarchy and the wider priesthood of the worldwide church offered the ideal justification to ease him out. Not wanting to arouse yet more controversy, he himself cited health reasons. That he lived another ten years reveals clearly enough that this was merely an excuse.

Though with some justification, the abuse scandal, too, was mostly a ruse. His predecessor John Paul II, as beloved as is his memory, had not solved the problem, nor has his successor in the years since. The glaring truth is that Catholicism, like most segments and denominations of Christendom, had found a way to live in comfortable alliance with the world's progressivism. It did not want its pope being so vocal about the sins of the world's deviant cultural shifts. The church must "get along" with the culture, not point fingers of challenge. Therefore Benedict had to go.

Thus, sooner than anyone would have predicted, it was suddenly time to elect a new pope. It was obvious to some that he would not be one to follow in Benedict's conservative and challenging footsteps.

A Plea to the Church on Behalf of Truth

It was not obvious to Catholic Deacon Keith Fournier. In an impassioned appeal, he implored the College of Cardinals in 2013 to stay the course for truth. Reflecting on Benedict's brief eight-year reign, and the suddenly imminent future, and echoing the historic significance of the moment, Fournier wrote:

> My readers know I believe that Benedict's years of service will be judged as having great significance. So too will the years of his predecessor, . . .
>
> The eyes of the world turn again to the eternal city where another papal conclave will soon begin. . . . [T]his election has far more significance than the one which occurred last year in the United States. Who will step into the shoes of the fisherman? What manner of man will he be? What will it mean for the Church? What will it mean for the world? . . .

Blessed John Paul II . . . helped to expose and bring down communism . . . . Pope Benedict XVI had taken on an ideological adversary even more dangerous; one with the potential to enslave millions in its deadly wake. That enemy was labeled by Joseph Cardinal Ratzinger before he assumed the Chair of Peter as the Dictatorship of Relativism. . . .

Pope Benedict XVI tried to guide the flock of Christ toward . . . mature faith. . . .

However, the dictatorship of relativism is a voracious vacuum . . . . It is an ideology of nihilism and despair. It threatens the very existence of the human person because it denies the existence of any values which can make us human or undergird the charity necessary for a common life. . . .

The next Pope has to continue the work of his predecessors. However, he also has to confront another "ism." One which has removed its sword from its sheath and declared war on the Church and her rightful role in culture. That adversary is militant secularism. I am not speaking of a secular state . . . .

Rather, I am speaking of the intolerant, anti-Christian, anti-religious secularism which is behind the growing effort to marginalize the Church and her institutions by attempting to keep her message and her mission within the buildings which she uses and out of the public square. The struggle we face in an increasingly hostile western culture involves a clash of worldviews, personal and corporate, and competing definitions of human freedom, human dignity, and human flourishing. The Catholic Church is at the center of that struggle.

We need to see our struggle in light of our own Christian history. . . . We need to engage the dictatorship of relativism which claims there are no truths and insist that there is Truth, it can be known—and it must govern our lives. This means facing persecution. Our path is already paved with the insults, accusations and calumny of our fellow citizens. It will get worse.

We are accused of being against progress and anti-science for defending the dignity of every human life—including the lives of our first neighbors in the womb. Nothing could be further from the truth. We are Pro-life because it is right. Science exists to serve the person, the family and the common good. In an age deluded by the architects of a cultural order of death we will never compromise on the truth concerning the dignity of every human life from conception through natural death. Science confirms what our conscience confirmed, those little girls and boys in the womb are our neighbors. It is always wrong to intentionally kill our innocent neighbors. To say and do otherwise is barbaric.

We insist that true marriage and family have been inscribed by the Divine Architect into the order of the universe. . . . Truth does not change, people and cultures do; sometimes for good and sometimes for evil. Marriage is the first society into which children are to be born, learn to be fully human, grow in virtue, flourish and take their role in families and communities. We must not be afraid to make the claim that children have a right to a mother and a father. They do.

Of course we care about the single parent family and the many broken homes. However, their existence does not change the norm necessary for a stable and healthy society. We must be careful not to be sucked in by those who play on our heart-strings. . . . [M]arriages and families are the glue of a healthy and happy social order. We need to be a visible, palpable reflection of this truth about marriage and family in our own lives. To live a faithful marriage is now countercultural.

Our convictions and claims concerning life and marriage are not outdated notions of a past era but provide the path to the future. We are the true progressives of every age. We insist upon the existence of a Natural Moral Law which can be known by all men and women through the exercise of reason. This is not only a Christian position. It is the ground upon which every great civilization has been built. It is the source for every great and authentic human and civil rights movement. The Natural Law gives us the moral norms we need to build societies and govern ourselves. It must also inform our positive law or we will become lawless and devolve into anarchy.

The next Pope will be a man who can expose the lie at the root of militant secularism and offer the only antidote, the new and true humanism of Christianity. I pray that he will be able to do so with the kind of joy and confidence which characterized the public ministry of Jesus.[1]

The College of Cardinals did not heed Deacon Fournier's counsel.

In March of 2013, nearly concurrent with President Obama's second inauguration, Pope Benedict was replaced by a kinder, gentler, less confrontational leader. The new pope was perfectly acceptable to progressivism. He would issue no challenges to its agenda.

Indeed, Pope Francis did the very opposite. In his first press conference as pope, when asked about homosexuals in the priesthood, he famously said, "If someone is gay and he searches for the Lord and has good will, who am I to judge?" His words, though falling short of official church teaching, in the minds of many, neutralized the instruction given by Pope Benedict. As a result homosexual men are now allowed in the Catholic priesthood. Benedict's stand against progressivism quickly became a distant memory.

For nearly four years, President Barack Obama and Pope Francis fittingly reigned in tandem, the titular heads of the world and the church spreading the sweetness and light of progressivism's ultimate triumph around the globe.

Meanwhile, Pope Emeritus Benedict lived for the next nine years in something like exile within the Vatican, ignored as an anachronism from the past by a Catholicism rushing headlong to embrace progressivism along with the rest of the world.

The two recent popes chose names that could not have more perfectly suited their outlooks, worldviews, and visions of the church and the world: *Benedict* and *Francis.*

The former decried the evils of a world consumed in its sin. As a true shepherd following in the footsteps of his sixth-century namesake, he courageously called the church to come out from the world and be separate.

The latter, also like his namesake, beloved St. Francis of Assisi of the thirteenth century, loves all living things and sees wonderful good in the world. He issues no challenges that might be perceived as negative. He judges no one and urges the church to embrace all the world's people in love and harmony.

Under Pope Francis, who has done for the church what Obama did for the United States, Catholicism's priesthood and people are happy to condone abortion, gays in the priesthood, and the normalization of much of the LGBTQ agenda. The challenge to righteousness, obedience, purity, and truth has disappeared from the Catholic landscape under Benedict's successor. The dictatorship of relativism sits on Catholicism's throne.

Benedict's legacy leaves us with two profound lessons.

The first is simply the powerful example of his courage to say, "Here I stand." We may not have the opportunity, in the words of Psalm 119, to speak of God's statutes before kings and world leaders as Benedict did. But we can follow him courageously to stand for virtue in our own corners of the world, to live and speak virtue to ourselves and to the world around us, and to pray to God, *Give me understanding. May I wholeheartedly follow your decrees. Make me wiser than my enemies. Let no sin rule over me. I hate and detest falsehood, but I love your law.*

Verily God gave Benedict understanding and made him wiser than his enemies. With all the faults that his critics laid at his charge, even perhaps for his papal ineffectiveness, Benedict detested the falsehoods of progressivism. May we righteously detest them also.

His life also gives us an ominous warning. We may *not* change the world. Recovering virtue in our own lives and in our corners of the world may not be enough to stop America's slide. As I write in late 2022 only days after November's midterm election, the news was announced that the Progressive Party has kept its control of the U.S. Senate.

In spite of hugely and overly optimistic hopes by the Traditional Party, progressivism rolls on. Nor is it likely that virtue will stop it. I fully expect in my lifetime to see permanent progressive majorities in both chambers of Congress and in the Supreme Court that will be unassailable.

The contest for virtue is not a political war. That war was lost a long time ago when a majority of fragmented worldly Christians, liberal men and women, and secular Catholics closed their eyes and—knowing all three trends were wrong—did not rise in integrity to object to progressivism's anti-Christianity then consented to the horrors of abortion and remained silent in face of the depravity of the LGBTQ agenda. As long as Christians (evangelicals and Catholics and Orthodox, liberals and conservatives) remain asleep to integrity, and blind to their fragmented hypocrisy for meekly and mutely accepting these three pillars of progressivism, the cultural wars will remain lost.

Individuals, however, *can* still win the ideological war, one step for virtue at a time. They can win that war for virtue and integrity within themselves.

That is all any of us can do—take our own steps higher into virtue and hope a few of those whose lives we may quietly influence will come along.*

A tribute to Pope Benedict XVI in the words of King David:

---

* I had hoped to send a copy of this book to former Pope Benedict. Sadly, he died on the last day of 2022. His legacy will live on.

I will also speak of thy testimonies before kings, . . . Thy statutes have been my songs . . . .

[W]ith my whole heart I keep thy precepts; . . . [G]ive me understanding that I may learn thy commandments. . . . Thy commandment makes me wiser than my enemies, for it is ever with me. I have more understanding than all my teachers, for thy testimonies are my meditation. I understand more than the aged, for I keep thy precepts. I hold back my feet from every evil way, in order to keep thy word. . . .

I hate every false way. . . . [L]et no iniquity get dominion over me. . . .

I hate and abhor falsehood, but I love thy law. . . .

My tongue will sing of thy word, for all thy commandments are right.

— Psalm 119:46a, 54a, 69b, 73b, 98–101, 128b, 133b, 163, 172

– PART 2 –

Disengaged Engagement Strategies

28

Disengaged Engagement:
PRACTICAL STRATEGIES FOR UPHOLDING VIRTUE

Throughout the writing of this book, as she has helped me think through various sections, my wife, Judy, has reminded me: "It's all good and right and true, but you need to give people practical, down-to-earth help in applying these principles. We know the situation is bad. But what do we actually *do* in the day-to-day to stand for virtue, to stand for our country, to live alertness, preparedness, attentiveness, authenticity, intellectual virtue, and everything else you discuss? How do we respond to people? What do we say? How do we handle ourselves in conversation? What do we do when hearing falsehoods spoken? It's got to mean more than being kind and nice and avoiding pointless arguments. Of course kindness is the foundation, but there have to be other definite things I can do that will make a difference."

Then she added, more personally yet, "I know you are writing for thousands of others out there. But you are also writing for *me*. I want to know what I should do to apply all this—when I go to work at the hospital, when I'm talking with people, when I'm alone, when I'm with Christians, when I'm with progressives. Today, tomorrow, next week—where you and I live."

The insight of her questions pinpointed the problem we all have—how to *live* the principles and truths we believe in. We easily fall into the trap of thinking we can change the world with bumper stickers. We approach politics and religion by plastering slogans, wearing buttons, handing out tracts and leaflets, and engaging in discussions to persuade people to our views and perspectives.

But virtue is immune to all those tactics.

Virtue is not a belief. It cannot be persuaded *into* anyone by any such external means. It cannot be accepted or adopted as an article of faith. Agreeing to the idea of virtue as a good thing accomplishes little. This may be a starting point but *only* a starting point. Virtue is a quality of character. It grows and develops and matures *internally* by lifestyle practice and work.

These next chapters, then, I am mostly writing for us—for Judy and me. My foremost responsibility and challenge is to live these principles myself. None of this is any good unless *I* internalize it. At the same time, I'm trying to see the big picture how *all* of us collectively can make a difference for virtue. In writing a book, I have to step outside myself too. I'm no politician, but if any group of men and women in our country need to have a strategy to apply these principles, it is those in the political arena. So I recognize the need to anticipate the questions of practicality they, like Judy, might also ask if this book should chance to find its way into any such hands. If others find these broader applications helpful, I can only invite them to join in the ideological war where each of them lives, just as Judy and I have to do so where we live.

Principles Will Guide Us More Than Specifics

At the end of his *How Should We Then Live?* (1976), Francis Schaeffer attempted to visualize the world of the future and offered predictions of numerous possibilities. Because he looked toward trends more than specific details, much in the final chapters of that book is amazingly insightful a generation and a half later. Some of it is summarized in appendix 2.

Yet that was forty years ago. Ronald Reagan was president, and the Berlin Wall was still in place. Though undergirded with his usual wisdom, many of his predictions now seem anachronistic. This highlights the pitfall of trying to be too specific. Whatever one says today may be outdated a year from now. Anything I offer about living in today's culture may become irrelevant if the ideological climate takes a dramatic turn two years from now that no one saw coming.

Suggestions and recommendations are likewise impossible to entirely transfer from one person's circumstances to another's. Some suggest that Christians ought to withdraw from the world into communities and make dramatic lifestyle changes. Actually, I don't disagree. Judy and I reflected on that very thing for many years, but no practical situation presented itself. We had a business to run. Now we are living in a gated residential neighborhood surrounded mostly by elderly non-Christians in a city that lies at the very heart of the nation's progressivism. Making a move to a Christian community in the country far from the world's pace is out of the question. Neither do most people have the finances that enable them to contemplate such radical lifestyle changes. Agreement in principle may still not translate to being practically able to do certain things.

We must discover *principles,* not always specifics. Principles are always a more reliable guide. Even the specifics I mention here are meant to point toward *principles* each will apply in different ways— the politician and plumber, the pastor and priest. That's another way of saying everyone has to write his or her own final chapters of the book. You have to discover your *own* strategies. My specifics or Aleksandr Solzhenitsyn's or former Pope Benedict's will not be yours.

I have chosen to write a book as one element of my taking a stand for truths I believe in. Maybe you will write a book too. Maybe you won't. But we all have to write for ourselves these last chapters of practical strategies.

I will therefore try to give some overarching thoughts I hope will personalize for serious Christians and Americans the virtues we have been talking about, hoping these will keep the general principles relevant well into the future.

Disengaged Engagement

I call the strategy I attempt to employ one of "disengaged engagement."

By this I reference the commands of both Old and New Testaments for Jews and Christians to live as a separate and distinct people. Followers of both faiths are commanded to live apart from the world and its people, to function separate from its entire value system, outlook, priorities, and lifestyles. This is an incumbent and commanded *requirement* of the Christian and Jewish faiths—not an optional sideline for only the most dedicated or, some might say, fanatical.

Judaism has historically obeyed this separation requirement more faithfully than has Christendom. But in our time, the vast majority of Jews and Christians intermingle with the world so completely that no one can tell the difference. I say this without judgment, simply pointing out that true Christianity and true Judaism that is rooted in the Old Testament *require* us to walk differently and apart from what the world says and does. What does being a Christian or a Jew mean to those who choose to disregard this fundamental separateness-tenet of both world faiths?

I must ask that same question of myself. When I look in the mirror, where might I be just as guilty of disregarding some command that is placed on *me,* as is the Christian woman who denies her faith by having an abortion? Where am I equally guilty of denying my faith without thinking about it?

We are called to be a people set apart, or as Jesus phrased it, "*in* but not *of* the world." How does the complicity of so many with progressivism's agenda fit with *not being of the world*? I suppose the answer to my question is, most Jews and Christians don't care much about that requirement anymore.

Yet while being distinct and (supposedly) walking according to different values and priorities and truths that the world cannot understand, we are at the same time also called to *influence* and engage the world for good, for righteousness, for virtue.

Finding that difficult balance, of course, has been the Achilles heel of Christianity for two thousand years. In most eras, Christians have not succeeded very well. They have erred by trying to be *too* engaged and thinking they can take over the world for Christianity (Constantine and Calvin and Oliver Cromwell all made that mistake). Or they have withdrawn into cloisters of diverse kinds, leaving the world to fend for itself and cutting themselves off from it completely.

Neither extreme works. Extremism at either pole is not what Jesus and other great spiritual leaders throughout history have exampled. We cannot change the intrinsic *worldliness* of the world. The Calvin strategy will always fail because the world will always be the world. Progressivism will never die. But we can *influence* the world as salt and light in the midst of its worldliness.

In my book on the commands of the Old Testament, I said that the Israelites were called to live "as a manifestly distinct righteousness-choosing people." That is a mouthful. But if you reflect on it a moment, you will see that phrase plunging to the very heart of things. It gives us our daily marching orders as a people attempting to live *in* but who are not *of* the world.

We are to be distinct—that is separate.

Disengaged.

At the same time we are to be "manifestly" distinct—that is *visible*, seen, noticed, not hidden away, and influential in the midst of our separateness.

Engaged.

What is described in the following pages may not be everyone's strategy. We have to disengage and engage each in our own ways. As I have reflected on this balance for many years, six general principles have risen to prominence in my thinking, along with some specifics that may flow out of them in different circumstances.

29

Disengaged Engagement Strategies: PRINCIPLE 1: VIRTUE IS INTERNAL

I cannot change the world. I can't change any man or woman other than myself. No one will be changed by my telling them, "Be virtuous." Putting a sign on our front lawn, "Vote for Virtue," will not influence the culture a hair's breadth. None of my neighbors will suddenly decide to order their lives by virtue as a result.

Virtue Is Defined by Personal Character and Is Invisibly Catching

The only impact I can have on another individual, on my neighbors, or upon the world is by being a man of virtue myself—a whole man, an integrated man, with all the parts of my being pointed in the same direction as a unity, my motives single-mindedly set toward virtue as a life goal. That inner orientation must be followed by my living as a manifestly distinct individual whose beliefs order his lifestyle. If virtue is not *visible*, no one will give heed to what I say.

I will never achieve that objective perfectly. I will never completely exhibit virtue. People who know me personally may say, "Huh, he's no one special. He doesn't seem all that virtuous. He's just an ordinary guy."

We're *all* ordinary men and women. I am a flawed man like all men, with my own range of personal weaknesses. But if my motives are set, then I will be generally moving in the right direction in life, flaws and all. We're ordinary people trying to live virtue in our ordinary lives. Most of us will not become popes or presidents. Wherever we are, we live a complex mix of virtue and unvirtue.

My first and foremost calling, therefore, is to develop virtue in my *own* life—not study it but *live* by the principles of virtue. Everything proceeds out of that foundation.

If my life, and its virtue or its unvirtue, happens to impact anyone, it will be transmitted like COVID. Both virtue and unvirtue are *catching*. And, like a virus, *invisibly* catching.

This has *many* implications. Everything that follows emerges out of that principle. Should anyone think the practicalities below are anything less than *utterly* pragmatic, try living these six simple points—especially the last—for a single day without lapsing into unvirtue.

It is *difficult* to live by virtue. It takes dedication to principles completely foreign to the world. It takes swimming upstream, against the current. That is hard work.

Principle 1 Practicalities

- My virtue-character is my only business.
- The internal mirror is my daily workshop for world change.
- The virtue-character of others is *not* my business. More important yet:
- The *unvirtue*-character of others (neither Trump, nor Biden or Pelosi, nor my irritating coworker, teacher, boss, parent, or aunt) is *especially* none of my business. Hence:
- Silence about others, except when offering praise of one known personally as exampling virtue, is usually the best policy.*

---

* I have admittedly spoken critically about certain public figures and their views and policies in an attempt to help us see the ideological war with clarity. I recognize my doing so may seem to go against this principle of silence. These are difficult tightropes to walk,

- Minding my own business therefore is today's first step, if not to change the world then at least, maybe in some way I may never see, my little corner of it—living virtue that someone else may catch because of some tiny word, deed, or expression of kindness and love they observed in me.

Should anyone take up the challenge of living by the virtue of minding their own business, Thomas à Kempis's words remind us powerfully to look in that virtue mirror twice a day:

Live a life adorned with virtue. Renew your purpose and stir yourself up daily.
Diligently search into and set in order both the outward and the inward man.
Continually recollect yourself, fix your good purpose every morning,
and every night examine how you have behaved in word, deed, and thought.[1]

---

especially when one is speaking in the public square about critically important public issues. I readily admit that my words challenge me too.

213

30

Disengaged Engagement Strategies
PRINCIPLE 2: INDIVIDUAL ACTIVISM

Jesus didn't try to change the political or contemporary world. He did not march on Rome or endorse candidates for Caesar or the Roman senate. Neither did he try to change the religious world. He didn't march in front of Herod's palace with placards or endorse anyone for king of Judea.

Politics and Culture Can Only Be Influenced Personally

Jesus gave his life to change the inner and personal world of *individual* men and women. He started with twelve men. Others caught the virus because they saw something in Jesus that drew them. They wanted the life they saw in him, as he offered it. He told them how they could have the same life he had. More caught the virus. The twelve grew to seventy, then hundreds, then thousands. Jesus spoke to crowds, but he was always speaking to *individuals* in those crowds about being people of a certain sort—men and women of spiritual virtue. Jesus changed the world not by political activism but by *individual activism,* the activism of virtue lived and passed on.

From that beginning, he and those who followed him did change the world. But they did not change it in the world's way using the world's methods. They changed it his way, virtue passed on one virtue-hungry soul at a time.

Principle 2 Practicalities

- Spread the seeds of virtue as Jesus did, individually and invisibly one seed at a time.
- Do not be deceived into thinking that institutional religion can spread virtue. Once it began to embrace the world's methods, Christendom became an institution. Virtue as its undergirding foundation and reason for being was lost. Even if you are in a church, virtue-spreading is still individual.
- If you feel called to engage in the ideas of the ideological war, find ways to do so individually, one-on-one, and only with hungry hearts. Megaphones are not the tool of individual activism, but quiet individual encounters where civility leads the way.
- Make John 3 your model for world change. Few conversations have changed the world more effectively than that recounted in John 3. It was a quiet conversation, at night, away from the spotlight, a one-on-one conversation between two men— one of them with a hungry heart. No mass rally or crusade ever changed the world so mightily as that quiet conversation between Jesus and a man named Nicodemus, who was privileged to hear those immortal words, "For God so loved the world . . . ."
- Be suspicious when progressivism's agenda is couched in spiritual terms or justified for spiritual reasons. Never forget: that at its core modernism hates Christianity and hates it most when dedicated men and women try to *live* their Christianity. Modernism is committed to Christianity's eradication from the public square.
- Be prepared to call out the hypocrisy of progressivism's ideas when its adherents attempt to co-opt, misrepresent, and twist Christianity's truths to justify purposes *contrary* to what Jesus

actually taught. Do so quietly and civilly. Though John 3 remains the model, Jesus called out the Scribes and Pharisees for their hypocrisy even though their hearts were *not* hungry. How to balance his Nicodemus strategy and his Pharisee strategy is, of course, the great difficulty and the great challenge.

- Quietly, unobtrusively, and civilly, reject the lie that progressivism and Christianity are compatible. Jesus was no progressive.
- Be wary of the value of huge events. Rallies, whether spiritual or political, may be an exercise in futility where few virtue seeds are likely to be planted.*

---

* There are exceptions to everything, and Billy Graham certainly represents the wonderfully virtuous exception to this recommendation. He was a planter of millions of virtue-seeds.

31

Disengaged Engagement Strategies
PRINCIPLE 3: THE FALSE ALLURE OF POLITICS

The ideological battle is one of spiritual values, not winning elections. I may vote, but I must be under no illusions. Virtue cannot be legislated or commanded upon a nation by executive fiat. Many have tried it through history. *All* have failed. Virtue cannot be imposed; it must be *caught*, virtue sprouting from the spread of many invisible seeds, growing to flourish in virtue's garden then passing on their own seeds as the garden quietly expands.

Public Activism Cannot Permanently Change
Politics and Culture

Politics is a singularly ineffective means for developing virtue or for spreading those invisible seeds. The ideological war will neither be fought nor won on the political battlefield.

The battlefield is the multitude of places where ordinary people like you and me engage with falsehood, deceit, and ungodliness—the world where millions of us take our daily stands for virtue in ways few will ever see.

We may cast political votes as wisely as we can. In doing so, however, we must remain conscious that inside the voting booth there are no opportunities to pass on the virtue-virus.

This principle, too, has many implications.

Principle 3 Practicalities

- Avoid the tantalizing and deceptive allure that politics is the answer to the world's problems.
- Never lose sight of John Calvin's great blunder—thinking Christianity, virtue, morality, and righteousness could be enforced by governmental decree and that "the world" could be turned into a *Christian* state.
- Never lose sight of Constantine's great blunder—thinking that national Christianity could make men, or a nation or empire, righteous.
- Never lose sight of Islam's fundamental falsehood—that such a thing as a "holy war" exists. It does *not* exist for Islam, for Christianity, for Republicans, for Democrats. In the ideological war, the only opponent is falsehood, not people.
- Political stumping, blogging, posting, meme-ing, tweeting, or discussion involving personalities rather than issues will not spread the virtue-virus.
- If you are a politician, begin every day by looking into the internal mirror and saying to the one staring back at you, "May I live *truth* today, not politics."
- If you are a politician, determine henceforth to stand up for truth and virtue—not your opinion, not what your party tells you, not what you are pressured to say or do.
- If you are a politician, consider resignation or changing your party affiliation to Independent.
- If you are a politician, cultivate equal friendships on both sides of the aisle.
- If you are a progressive, listen to the logic and common sense of your conservative brethren.

- If you are a politician, ferret out hypocrisy from the positions you have espoused—whether abortion or gun control, whether taxes or gay rights, whether immigration or social justice. Root out your inconsistencies and stand for virtue.
- If you are a politician, determine never again to vote the party line *because* it is the party line. If you are voted out of office, so, after a fashion, was Pope Benedict. Among those (perhaps few) who understand the courage to stand for truth that drove him, his legacy will endure. Build your legacy with similar courage. No legacy of courage ever read, "He went with the flow." What do you want your tombstone to read? *He/She was a loyal politician*, or *he/she was an individual of virtue and integrity.*

32

Disengaged Engagement Strategies
PRINCIPLE 4: REFUSE TO LIVE BY LIES

Rod Dreher summarized Aleksandr Solzhenitsyn, and I summarize his summarization. Solzhenitsyn says that he or she who refuses to live by lies will not:

- say or write or affirm or distribute anything that distorts the truth;
- participate in any collective action unless he truly believes in the cause;
- take part in a meeting or discussion that is closed and not open to the truth;
- vote for an unworthy candidate;
- support journalism that distorts or hides facts; and
- remain at an event or in a discussion when he hears lies, ideological drivel, or propaganda.

Dreher concludes, "'This is by no means an exhaustive list of the possible and necessary ways of evading lies,' Solzhenitsyn writes. 'But he who begins to cleanse himself will, with a cleansed eye, easily discern yet other opportunities.'"[1]

Walking in Quiet Courage, Integrity, Valor, and Truth

The bulleted points above were written for another time, specifically addressing political activism during the Cold War. We may not personally endorse them all. But the underlying principles are ones we can translate from Solzhenitsyn's different circumstances into our own. If we are not at a political event but merely drawn into a discussion at school or around the water cooler at work or are watching the news on television, our application may be to walk away from the discussion, turn off the TV, or stop watching the major news networks altogether.

Therefore, we can add to Solzhenitsyn's list.

Principle 4 Practicalities

- Don't be eager to speak your mind when you hear untruth spoken.
- Resist airing your views to a hostile audience. You will convince no one.
- Quietly and unobtrusively assess the open-mindedness of those with whom you regularly cross paths.
- Only air your views when you sense a potential open heart and mind.
- In the company of the closed-minded, keep silent.
- With the open-minded, find quiet and unobtrusive ways to express your convictions without challenging and criticizing anyone. When speaking to Nicodemus, Jesus did not bring up the hypocrisy of the Pharisees (though he did on other occasions). To Nicodemus's hungry heart, he spoke only truth.
- Find quiet and unobtrusive ways to *listen*.
- Be very careful when you feel led to speak, that you are not really just itching for a verbal brawl.
- Even if you say nothing, do not convey by silent body language of approval that you agree with lies spoken by progressives. You don't have to scowl, but truth must out even if nonverbally.

- Speak your convictions briefly, succinctly, and thoughtfully—never emotionally.
- Don't explain your convictions or ramble to justify them. Explanations breed debate and argumentation.
- If asked why about an idea you have expressed, repeat your conviction but *do not elaborate.* Answering the why with a long explanation will inevitably result in a critical counter-argument—and a pointless debate has begun. Do *not* try to explain. If anything, counter with a probing question of your own.
- Don't vocalize your views to the *air*, glancing about hoping someone is listening.
- Don't vocalize your views to a group unless you can speak to one open-minded individual with whom you can establish eye contact and with whom you sense a personal connection and genuine interest.
- When detecting opposition to anything you are saying, and you feel counter arguments brewing, go silent.
- Never engage in argumentation or debate about potentially heated or controversial topics or political perspectives.
- Don't be fearful of nonconformity. Wear nonconformity toward the culture of political correctness like a badge of honor—quiet, dignified, holding your head high.

With great perception, George MacDonald cut straight to the heart of the difficult balance:

> Is our life, then, a witnessing to the truth? . . . Are we careful to be true? . . . When contempt is cast on the truth, do we smile? Wronged in our presence, do we make no sign that we hold by it? I do not say we are called upon to dispute, and defend with logic and argument, but we are called upon to show that we are on the other side. But when I say *truth*, I do not mean *opinion*: to treat opinion

as if that were truth, is grievously to wrong the truth. The soul that loves the truth and tries to be true, will know when to speak and when to be silent; but the true man will never look as if he did not care. We are not bound to say all we think, but we are bound not even to look what we do not think.[2]

33

Disengaged Engagement Strategies
PRINCIPLE 5: TAKE STANDS WITH COURAGE AND CARE

When they began producing films extolling the LGBTQ agenda, I wrote to Hallmark and canceled our subscription. Their cowardice ruined the tradition of Hallmark Christmas movies for us. True, as an author of fiction who loves complex plots and engaging growing characters, I could only take a few every year! Still, it was a tradition we looked forward to. Hallmark's lack of courage to stand up to the pressure of a tiny LGBTQ minority, I fear, roused not civility but anger in my heart. About the same time, I also canceled our subscription to the Disney Channel. One expects it from Disney, but Hallmark's cowardice was a blow.

Be Respectfully and Humbly Bold,
Always Preserving the Human Brotherhood

I had long delayed taking action on something gnawing at the back of my brain for some time. Writing this chapter finally brought me fully awake to my own inconsistency. It is a small point but one where I took my stand and lived up to my own words.

I have a dear relative who has sent a Starbucks gift card to me every Christmas for several years. I have enjoyed using them but also know that Starbucks supports every tenet of the progressive agenda. It uses profits in ways that directly contradict everything I believe. For too long I have allowed them to use my business (or that of my generous relative!) to encourage and support the decline of the moral fabric of our nation.

We find our own personal ways to fight the ideological war and stand for truth. I, too, must heed Solzhenitsyn's words and live not by lies. I intended to mount no campaign, but I felt that I needed to stand more consistently with my own personal belief system.

Therefore, I wrote the following letter. It served two purposes: removed a tiny thimbleful from the ocean of Starbucks' coffers and made a small stand, hopefully in good taste, with civility and kindness, to be complicit and silent no longer.

> Dear ——,
>
> This is a long overdue letter to thank you for the Starbucks gift cards you have been faithfully sending every year at Christmas. We really like Starbuck's coffee, overpriced as it is, and your cards made the periodic treat possible. We especially enjoyed it when driving back and forth to Eureka. We had our special places where we stopped and always looked forward to it. They also made perfect bathroom stops!
>
> However, I have recently become deeply convicted about supporting Starbucks when their publicly progressive policies are so opposed to everything I believe as a Christian. As a liberal company, they stand against much of what Jesus taught, notably the sanctity of life and the sanctity of marriage.
>
> Therefore, as much as I have enjoyed and appreciated them, I feel as a Christian I need to make a stand. Therefore, I'm going to ask you to send me no more Starbucks gift cards. You can substitute something else . . . or nothing at all! Knowing you is all the gift I need!

Thank you for understanding,
Much love, and God's best to you and the whole family.

Hallmark won't care. Disney won't care. Starbucks won't care. But I have to look in the mirror. And I care.

Principle 5 Practicalities

- If you're in a church that condones abortion or same-sex marriage, leave that church. Quietly and courteously take your stand for truth, make your decision known, then walk away. Don't argue or try to change your church. Argumentation will persuade no one.
- If you're in a denomination that endorses gay or lesbian clergy, leave it. If appropriate let those close to you know of your decision and why you have made it, then walk away. Don't argue.
- If your pastor or priest preaches politics rather than obedience to the commands of the New Testament, leave the church.
- Don't be wedded to Sunday church attendance above the truth. Better to attend no church than a church where the truth is not taught.
- If you find yourself drawn into an argument, respectfully go silent. In a friendly and courteous spirit, excuse yourself and walk away.
- Use any means possible to take your children out of public school. It is the greenhouse of progressive values and a destructive, humanity-killing worldview.
- *Especially* if your son or daughter is in a public school where sex education or gender falsehoods are being taught, get them out. Only an unthinking parent allows his or her children to be sacrificed to the Moloch of the culture's falsehoods and indoctrinated into the gender-lies of progressivism. You *must* protect your children.

- If you have work conflicts in a progressive environment and you feel the culture's lies getting inside you and influencing *you* negatively rather than giving you opportunity to spread the virtue-virus, investigate alternate employment options that will not have that effect.
- If your job requires going against your conscience, investigate alternate employment options that will not do so.
- If you're watching a movie or program extolling gay or lesbian characters, turn it off.
- If you feel so led, you may choose to stop supporting businesses that are feeding progressivism's lies subtly into the general culture.
- Don't watch or read biased news reporting from outlets spreading progressivism's propaganda.

34

Disengaged Engagement Strategies
PRINCIPLE 6: EVERYONE CAN SPREAD VIRTUE

It is such a simple principle yet may be life changing: someone may be watching and listening.

Invisible Virtue Seeds Have Impact

Planting verbal or visual seeds of virtue is usually unconscious, unplanned, unpredictable, nor may you ever know of it, nor know of the results. But seeds of truth sprout, send down roots, grow, and bear fruit.

The world is literally changed one virtue-seed at a time. May the Spirit of God and our own obedience make us faithful virtue-planters!

Principle 6 Practicalities

- Keep abreast of the ideological war. Don't fall asleep at the wheel.
- Read some of the titles mentioned in the footnote on page 65. Keep in mind that everyone approaches the culture wars from different vantage points. As I have tried to emphasize, look beyond specifics to overarching principles. Separating

from the world in family living, education, in the workplace, how and when to speak out boldly, resisting technology and social media, and many other topics addressed in other books are timely and relevant. But they all have to be individually applied in the diverse range of circumstances in which we find ourselves.

- You may also want to read my series Tribulation Cult, the fictional companion to *Endangered Virtues.*
- Don't use this book as a tract or give it to the closed-minded. Share it only with the virtue-hungry where it may be able to plant seeds.
- Get together with like-minded friends to discuss how to help and support one another in the ideological war. In this environment, free-flowing discussion is important. The purpose is not to isolate yourselves in echo chambers but to sustain and encourage your fellow foot soldiers in the dedication to uphold virtue.
- Seek communities of truth, not to confirm bias but as support systems spreading salt and light in the culture.
- Find men and women of virtue and wisdom and glean from them.
- Give careful thought and prayer to all the perspectives, outlooks, values, and practices by which you order your life. If your life has drifted into patterns of progressivism, take steps to change those patterns.
- Heed Thomas à Kempis's words as our marching orders every day:

> Arise and begin this very instant and say,
> "Now is the time to be doing . . . . Avoid small faults.
> Give yourself to inward things.
> Think what you are about."

Postscript

Sadly history has shown that most Christians are too apathetic to commit themselves to lives of virtue. In our present time, this is equally true of concerned Americans who see their country slipping away but are similarly too apathetic to take such stands as these.

How many does it take to change a culture?

It takes one—it takes many *ones*.

But every *one* step takes courage. And courage is hard.

THE VIRTUE DEBATE
OF OUR TIME

It is probably clear that I rely on the Bible as my truth-foundation. I use it to evaluate both spiritual ideas and political ideas. I do not look to the Bible with legalistic rigidity, which can lead to error as well as to truth. Rather, I rely on the Bible for its timeless wisdom. It is that wisdom I am constantly trying to plumb more perceptively. This appendix may mean little to those who do not value the Bible as a source of truth. But for Christians wrestling with changing cultural mores and ethics, hopefully this "postscript to virtue" will clarify a methodology for evaluating truth somewhat differently than that found in today's world.

Four Foundation Stones

Along with the Bible as my primary truth-foundation, I add three others. In my lifelong quest to understand life, the world, myself, and *truth*, I try to base my perspectives on these four fundamental building blocks.

1. The Bible.
2. The nature and character of God.

3. The purposes of God.
4. Common sense.

These foundations undergird everything about my outlook and my approach to life. When I am investigating any quandary, I try to shine light onto the question through these four windows. These are the grids I use to assess cultural and political and personal truth as well as spiritual truth.

Thinking about abortion, for example, which I call the virtue debate of our time, these four factors offer more clarity than all the political arguments brought to bear on the matter in fifty years. These foundation stones are eminently *practical*. I offer that perspective neither as a pro-choice liberal nor a pro-life conservative but as a *Christian* man who tries to assess right, wrong, and truth according to these four factors.

Yet these four guidelines are as slippery as biblical literality. People infuse not only the Bible but also the nature and purposes of God with widely differing interpretations. What appears common sense to one might look ridiculous to another. There will never be consensus on any of the four. All I can do is use them as wisely and objectively as I am capable of.

Clarifying my foundational approach further, I try to read the Bible *literally*, straightforwardly, intelligently, and with common sense. Not with *rigid* literality but with sensible and intelligent literality. That's why I prefer the term *straightforward* to *literal*. It is nothing more than applying Occam's razor to biblical interpretation—the principle which says that the most straightforward explanation usually points in a true direction. I only deviate from a straightforward reading when it seems to me that literality violates the character of God, the purposes of God, and common sense. I also have to bring objectivity to the table. I cannot start with an opinion then backtrack to mold the Bible's words to fit that opinion.

In summary, I take the Bible as it comes. I assume literality unless compelling reason exists to look at broader meanings. Then I try to draw common-sense, intelligent conclusions.

A Controversial Verse: Genesis 1:27

Let's jump into controversial waters.

Following the *creation* of the universe, Genesis 1:27 adds that God created humanity as "*male* and *female*."

Here we find ourselves in a region where there is no compelling reason to look beyond literality. In this case, the science of human biological anatomy perfectly backs up the Bible's literality. Science, in a sense, *proves* the biblical account of human sexual origins. Not the *how* of those origins but the binary *nature* of those origins. There is no scientific substitute reading of "male and female." Therefore, I read the text *literally*, as it comes. Science and the Bible say precisely the same thing—humanity was created as male and female.

What does modernity do with those words? *Male* and *female*—binary biological creation.

Many progressives argue that birth-sex and the functionality of gender is *not* binary. They do not believe it was created inviolate and unchangeable. That's their opinion. They assume their opinion must be true. They are unable to differentiate between *opinion* and *truth*, so they reject both science and the Bible in order to hold to their desired opinion.

There are the words in black and white. *Male* and *female*. Biological science confirms both words. There is no alternate reading of something different that the words *might* have been intended to mean—at least that I can see. Who knows what aberrant interpretations may be waiting in the future for someone to put forward. Therefore, there is no other way to read this verse than exactly as it reads, reflecting precisely what was the intended purpose of humanity's origin.

Common sense, too, along with human biology, supports the veracity of male and female binary creation. There are *two* human bodies and *only* two human bodies. Nothing can change the intrinsic nature of either.*

---

* Clearly physical abnormalities occur. Hermaphroditism is a reality—though obviously rare. No one is disputing that such physical rarities exist. But no reputable scientist denies that they are *ab*-normal.

The conclusion is unambiguous: biological sex is binary and unchangeable. That is an undeniable physical and scientific fact.

Circular reasoning cannot turn opinion into truth. Wanting something to be true cannot make it true. That everyone around us says it is true does not make it true. Political correctness and woke ideas do not make it true.

What Is God's Purpose?

Abortion provides an even more intriguing matter of debate because the science is not so straightforward as in the case of Genesis 1:27. No scientific *proof* exists that abortion is right or wrong. We have to look beyond proof—to ethics, morals, and personal desires. That's where it gets fuzzy.

Abortion is not a matter of science but of morality. Scientifically there is zero dispute that an unborn child/fetus/baby is *alive* immediately after conception, and alive in increasingly human ways even within days, surely within weeks. It's not a question, as is often said, of "when life begins." The science of *life* itself is not in dispute.

Science, therefore, does prove that human life exists before birth. But science does not address whether it is right or wrong to kill human life before it exits the womb. The only debatable point is whether it is right/legal/moral to artificially remove that life form, whatever one calls it, from a woman's body by her choice and put an end to that life.

Amid all the myriad talking and debating points on both sides, there is a simpler way to look at it. We return to the four foundation stones. There we must take a hard, careful, honest, and objective look at the purpose of God. At that point, abortion ceases to be a political, legal, or even a *personal* question. I cease to be a liberal or a conservative. It's not even a matter of ethics or right and wrong.

The only questions become: What are God's purposes? What did God *intend* when he created life?

Does any Christian who is being deeply honest with herself believe it is God's desire and *purpose* that a life he created be aborted? What can age—two weeks, two months, five months, seven months—have to do with that fundamental question? Life is life.

Is it God's *purpose* that life be terminated?

Once we start hair-splitting with questions such as, "But when is killing *actually* killing?" and then excuse abortion because it is not *really* killing, by then we've lost the plot. To use a Schaefferism, we have escaped from reason.

Many justifications are raised in support of abortion. This is no place to debate their pros and cons. I only ask whether abortion is included in God's purpose and plan It is a serious biblical, and for Christians an *eternal*, question. Can such be God's purpose and intent?

I realize many abortion advocates do not share this spiritual orientation. So let's take the Bible and God out of it altogether.

Does any honest, thinking *atheist* truly think the purpose of life and the universe—even an impersonal universe—is furthered by killing unwanted babies? They may have other reasons (such as population control) for supporting abortion. But none of those can be supported by the evolutionary argument. Population may need to be controlled, but killing unborns to justify sexual license is not the answer.

Do evolutionists believe that the flow and objective of evolution (even its *purpose* in a manner of speaking) is validated by abortion? Removing God from the picture, we might say evolution has determined that offspring are born in the animal kingdom when certain things happen. It is evolution's means to continue each species. Abortion obviously thwarts evolution's method.

If secularists believe so strongly in evolution, how are they also so vocal in support of a practice that works precisely *contrary* to evolution? If *proof* against the legitimacy of abortion exists, it seems that evolution itself provides it.

The extreme care taken to protect the fetal "life" of a pregnant endangered Panda bear raises so many inconsistencies and hypocrisies alongside the millions of unborn human lives snuffed out every year, it is almost pointless to draw the comparison. We can see the dichotomy clearly enough.

The fourfold foundational ethos upon which to base truth—the Bible, the nature and character of God, the purposes of God, and common sense—tells us on all four counts that something is wrong with this picture.

Abortion violates all four and violates the underlying purpose of evolution as well.

This conclusion is not directed at liberals any more than at conservatives, evangelicals, Catholics, and Christians who also support abortion in our time. Abortion is practiced throughout the political and social spectrum. This conclusion is an indictment against no group or political point of view but against abortion itself.

Is God Pleased?

Abortion is nothing less than a societal scourge that is an affront to God. Christian women who place their personal desires above God's clear intent, who favor the right of women to have abortions, or, worse, have abortions themselves, will one day have to face their Maker and give account of themselves. So will the men who supported them in those decisions. I cannot imagine any response other than the shame and remorse of bitter tears as they cry, "What have we done?! How could we have been so blind to the truth?!"

The culpability of non-Christians is not mine to wonder about. But surely the so-called Christian value system of millions of faithful church-attending men and women, who have so little regard for the purposes of God that they choose to support abortion, must be a faith void of reality.

What will they say to God?

What can they possibly say to justify going along with the world's great sin and for contributing to the extermination of entire future generations of God's precious little ones?

The future will look back on them with a condemnation even greater than that with which we look back to the slavery of our nation's early years. The outrage against them will be even greater. They will say of the women of our time and the men who urged them on—women and men who valued life so little, who made immoral decisions and compounded their poor choices by murdering the living fruit of their immorality—"There is no excuse for their sin. They lived in an enlightened time. They should have known better. Shame on them all. Shame on those who murdered the future."

That is not a "conservative" point of view. That is the conclusion of one for whom the purposes of God *matter*.

In one of his many wonderfully probing prayers, Thomas à Kempis wrote, "Grant me, O Lord, to know that which is worth knowing, to love that which is worth loving, to praise that which pleases you most, to esteem that highly which to you is precious."

Can we, as thinking Christians, believe that abortion is pleasing and precious to God?

Do liberal Catholic and Protestant and Orthodox women and men, do conservative women and men, do senators and congressmen and congresswomen, do whites and blacks, do Supreme Court justices, do presidents and vice presidents and future candidates, do governors and state legislators, do pastors and priests, do political newspersons and pundits, do Hollywood's actors and actresses—do any of these believe that abortion is pleasing and precious to God?

This is no question that can be answered on the basis of opinion. It is a question that turns on right and wrong, ethics, morality, and goodness. It is based even more fundamentally on *truth* and on the character of God himself.

Is God pleased?

Appendix 2

AN ORWELLIAN WARNING

The following, written toward the end of Francis A. Schaeffer's life, is remarkably prophetic for our own time almost half a century later.

> [I]f there are no absolutes . . . only one other alternative is left . . . an elite, giving authoritative arbitrary absolutes . . . . Society is left with . . . an elite filling the vacuum left by the loss of Christian consensus . . . in the West . . . .
>
> So far, two elites put themselves forward offering to fill the vacuum in our culture. The . . . New Left . . . . Then . . . an elite composed of intellectuals . . . .
>
> Daniel Bell (1919–), professor of sociology at Harvard University, . . . sees that in the final analysis the whole state—its business, its education, its government, even the daily pattern of the ordinary man's life—becomes a matter of control by the technocratic elite. They are the only ones who know how to run the complicated machinery of society and they will then, in collusion with the government elite, have all the power necessary to manage it.

Bell's most astute warning concerns the ethical implications . . . .

Humanism has led to its natural conclusion . . . . In our era . . . [h]umanists have been determined to beat to death the knowledge of God . . . and they have been determined to do this even though the death of values has come with the death of that knowledge.

We see two effects of our loss of meaning and values. The first is degeneracy . . . .

But we must notice that there is a second result of modern man's loss of meaning and values which is more ominous, and which many people do not see. This second result is that the elite . . . will offer us arbitrary absolutes, and who will stand in its way?

Will the silent majority (which at one time we heard so much about) help? The so-called silent majority was, and is, divided into a minority and a majority. The minority are either Christians who have a real basis for values or those who at least have a memory of the days when the values were real. The majority are left with only their two poor values of personal peace and affluence.

With such values, will men stand up for their liberties? Will they not give up their liberties step by step, inch by inch, as long as their own personal peace and prosperity is sustained and not challenged, and as long as the goods are delivered ? . . . Much of the church is no help here either, because for so long a large section of the church has only been teaching a relativistic humanism using religious terminology.

I believe the majority of the silent majority, young and old, will sustain the loss of liberties without raising their voices as long as their own life-styles are not threatened. And since personal peace and affluence are so often the only values that count with the majority, politicians know that to be elected they must promise these things. Politics has largely become not a matter of ideals—increasingly men and women are not stirred by the values of . . . truth—but of supplying a constituency with a frosting of personal peace and affluence. They know that voices will not be raised as long as people have these things, or at least an illusion of them.

Edward Gibbon (1737–94) in his *Decline and Fall of the Roman Empire (1776–88)* said that the following five attributes marked Rome at its end: first, a mounting love of show and luxury (that is, affluence); second, a widening gap between the very rich and the very poor . . . ; third, an obsession with sex; fourth, freakishness in the arts, masquerading as originality, and enthusiasms pretending to be creativity; fifth, an increased desire to live off the state. It all sounds so familiar. We have come a long road . . . and we are back in Rome.[1]

As we consider the coming of an elite, an authoritarian state, to fill the vacuum left by the loss of Christian principles, we must not think naively of the models of Stalin and Hitler. We must think of a manipulative authoritarian government. Modern governments have forms of manipulation at their disposal which the world has never known before . . . .

If man . . . is only the sum of the impersonal plus time plus chance . . . [o]ur own generation can thus disregard human life. On the one end we kill the embryo through abortion—and on the other end we will introduce euthanasia for the old. The one is already here and the door is opened for the other . . . .

Modern man has no boundary condition for what he should do; he is only left with what he can do. Moral "oughts" are only what is sociologically accepted at the moment . . . . All morals and law are seen as relative . . . .

In light of this discussion about social manipulation, three questions arise: First, who will control the controllers? Second, what will happen now that people have no boundary condition indicating what they should do in contrast to what they can do? Third, if mankind is only what modern people say it is, why does man's biological continuation have value? . . .

With an elite providing the arbitrary absolutes . . . the general apparatus of the mass media can be a vehicle for manipulation . . . . All that is needed is that the world-view of the elite and the world-view of the central news media coincide . . . . Their world-view is the grid which determines their presentation . . . .

Synthesis has won on both sides of the Iron Curtain: people see no fixed, final right or wrong, but only a mixture in public dealing as well as in private morals, in foreign affairs as well as in internal matters. This is especially so in the intellectuals who have understandingly carried the abandonment of the Christian base toward its logical conclusion. But it is also true of those who have been influenced by this thought without analyzing it . . . . Absolute principles have little or no meaning in the place to which the decline of Western thought has come . . . .

Winston Churchill's (1874–1965) words in the House of Commons after the Munich Pact was signed now sound prophetic: ". . . Do not suppose this is the end. This is only the beginning of the reckoning. This is only the first sip, the first foretaste of a bitter cup which will be proffered to us year by year unless, by a supreme recovery of moral health . . . we arise again and take our stand for freedom . . . ." . . .

But the years that have passed show no sign that such a lesson has been learned. Without the base for right and wrong . . . the weak humanistic ideals are not and will not be enough in our own generation or for the future . . . .

We are not excused from speaking, just because the culture and society no longer rests as much as they once did on Christian thinking . . . . Christians do not need to be in the majority in order to influence society.[2]

Appendix 3

HOW WISDOM GROWS

Not wanting to turn this book into a devotional treatise, I place the following in an appendix for those who may have read chapter 26 and asked, What can I do to cultivate the soil of personal character that will grow wisdom?

I do not offer the following points pretending to have all the answers to such a high truth as wisdom. One of my personal mentors pointed me in these directions many years ago. I offer them as having been extremely helpful to me in understanding and praying for wisdom.

1. *Point the inner compass of character toward God's North*—toward virtue, goodness, right, integrity, and truth. In other words, live the virtues. Wisdom begins with the direction one chooses to point the compass of motive, will, and character.

2. *Pray for wisdom.* If you desire wisdom, ask God to develop it in you. Ask him to show you his purposes. Ask him to give you eyes to see things as he sees them. Internalize this verse: "If any of you lacks wisdom, let him ask God who gives to all men generously , . . . and it will be given him" (James 1:5). Then pray the wisdom prayer: "God, develop wisdom within me. Give me your eyes to see myself, the world, and people as you see them."

3. *Discover ways to learn God's purposes.* The four Gospels from the New Testament are the clearest articulation of what it really means to see through God's eyes. That's what Jesus was doing all his life. In the Gospels, he told us what that looked like.

4. *Seek out men and women of wisdom and glean from them.* Sit silent in their presence and drink from the character of their years. Make men and women of virtue, integrity, and wisdom—the lifetime virtues— your personal mentors. Imbibe their character. They will rarely be found in the political realm. Many have walked the path toward wisdom before you, but they are becoming harder and harder to find in today's world. They will be the quiet ones who have lived long, good lives learning to see with God-eyes.

   This mentoring may be accomplished significantly through the writings of such men and women. All my spiritual mentors are now dead. About half of them were dead before I was born. They have mentored me in wisdom through their books.

It can be easy to mistake a quiet, soft-spoken personality with wisdom. It is true—silence is an attribute of wisdom and wisdom will preserve its grace in silence. But silence does not in itself reveal wisdom. It may simply reveal a soft-spoken, reticent individual whose silence may be hiding a seething repository of negativity, selfishness, judgment, and unforgiveness.

One of my mentors, Thomas à Kempis, whom I have quoted several times, wrote the following, as if foreseeing by half a millennium exactly how many perceptive men and women in future years would stand in relation to him: "Enquire willingly, and hear with silence the words of holy men."

The silence of wisdom is not a matter of personality but of having spent a lifetime learning to see with God's perspective and vision. It is the *chosen* silence of a loving, listening heart, as Kempis further says, that does not stand in its own conceits:

Be not wise in your own conceit.
Be united within yourself and inwardly single minded.
Do not be rash in your proceedings, nor stand stiffly in your own conceits.
Keep company with the humble and plain, the devout and virtuous.
Do not be too confident in your own opinion.

ENDNOTES

Chapter 1

1. C. S. Lewis, "Preface," *Mere Christianity* (New York: The Macmillan Publishing Co., Anniversary Edition, 1981), xlii-xliv, italics in the original.

2. C. S. Lewis, *Studies in Words* (London: Cambridge University Press, 1960), 7–8, italics in the original.

Chapter 2

1. Noah Webster, *First Edition of an American Dictionary of the English Language,* facsimile of 1828 ed. (Anaheim, CA: Foundation for American Christian Education, 1967), s.v. "virtue."

2. Webster, s.v. "vice."

Chapter 3

1. Francis Schaeffer, *The God Who Is There* (Downers Grove, IL: Intervarsity Press, 1968), 13–14.

2. Schaeffer, 14.

Chapter 5

1. Francis Schaeffer, *How Should We Then Live?* (Old Tappan, NJ: Fleming H. Revell, 1976), quoted from *The Collected Works of Francis A. Schaeffer,* vol. 5 (Westchester, IL: Crossway Books, 1982), 166.

2. Schaeffer, *How Should We Then Live,* 83–84.

Chapter 6

1. Pope Benedict XVI: "This attitude of resignation with regard to truth lies at the heart of the crisis of the West, the crisis of Europe. If truth does not exist for man, then neither can he ultimately distinguish between good and evil" (September 8, 2007, Mariazell, Austria).

Chapter 9

1. Rod Dreher, *The Benedict Option* (New York: Sentinel Books, Random House, 2017), 4, 8.
2. Dreher, 17.

Chapter 10

1. George MacDonald, "Love Thy Neighbour," *Unspoken Sermons, First Series* (London: Alexander Strahan, 1867), page numbers vary according to edition.

Chapter 14

1. Thomas Kelly, "The Simplification of Life," *A Testament of Devotion* (New York: Harper and Brothers, 1941), 113–14, italics in the original.

Chapter 15

1. Publication source unknown.
2. Publication source unknown.

Chapter 17

1. Rod Dreher, *Live Not by Lies* (New York: Sentinel Books, Random House, 2020), xiv–xv, 8, 30.
2. Keith M. Alber, "Opinion from a Former Judge," *The Epoch Times* (December 5, 2021). The original source and name of the textbook is unknown, so the authenticity of the quote cannot be verified. In his article, Alber wrote, "I am a student of law whose age is 85. My first year of college was 68 years ago. One class I took was political science. A half-page of my textbook essentially outlined a few steps to overturn a democracy."
3. Dreher, *Live Not by Lies*, 54, 8, 9, 17.

Chapter 18

1. During the 2016 presidential campaign Hillary Clinton used the phrase "basket of deplorables" to describe Donald Trump's supporters. At an LGBT campaign fundraising event in New York City on September 9, 2016, she said. "You know, to just be grossly generalistic, you could put half of Trump's supporters into what I call the basket of deplorables. They're racist, sexist, homophobic, xenophobic, Islamophobic—you name it."

2. During the 2008 presidential campaign, in a speech in San Francisco on April 6, 2008, candidate Barrack Obama said, "Our challenge is to get people persuaded that we can make progress when there's not evidence of that in their daily lives . . . . You go into some of these small towns in Pennsylvania, and like a lot of small towns in the Midwest, the jobs have been gone now for twenty-five years and nothing's replaced them . . . . And it's not surprising then they get bitter, they cling to guns or religion or antipathy to people who aren't like them or anti-immigrant sentiment or anti-trade sentiment as a way to explain their frustrations."

Chapter 19

1. Henry Drummond, *The Greatest Thing in the World: An Address*, a classic exposition on 1 Corinthians 13 (London: Hodder and Stoughton, 1890).

Chapter 20

1. C. S. Lewis, "The Humanitarian Theory of Punishment," *God in the Dock* (Grand Rapids: William B. Eerdmans, 1978), 292.

Chapter 21

1. Webster, s.v. "integrity."
2. Kelly, *A Testament of Devotion,* 114.

Chapter 25

1. Thomas à Kempis, *The Imitation of Christ* (1471), translated many times from the French and published in hundreds of editions, many of them old and in archaic language. The wordings of these selections are taken from various editions.

Chapter 26

1. Webster, s.v. "wisdom," italics in the original.

Chapter 27

1. Deacon Keith Fournier, "John Paul Took on Communism, Benedict Took on Relativism, Next Pope Must Take on Militant Secularism," *Year of Faith*, Catholic Online, March 1, 2013 (https://www.catholic.org/homily/

yearoffaith/story.php?id=49830); reprinted, "Daily Reading," November 13, 2022. Constitutional and human rights lawyer and clergy member Keith Fournier is founder and chairman of Common Good Foundation and Common Good Alliance. He is the former director of the American Center for Law and Justice.

Chapter 29

1. Kempis, *The Imitation of Christ.*

Chapter 32

1. Dreher, *Live Not by Lies,* 18; quote from Aleksandr Solzhenitsyn, "Live Not by Lies!" *The Solzhenitsyn Reader: New and Selected Writings, 1947–2005,* eds. Edward E. Erickson Jr. and Daniel J. Mahoney (Wilmington, DE: ISI Books, 2009), 559.

2. George MacDonald, "Kingship," *Unspoken Sermons, Third Series* (1889; repr., Eureka, CA: Sunrise Books, 1988), italics in the original.

Appendix 2

1. Schaeffer, *How Should We Then Live?,* 224–25, 226–27.
2. Schaeffer, 29, 235, 237, 239, 240–41, 249–50, 254.